READING WRITING

READING WRITING
Handwriting Analysis for Mentalists and Magicians

ARIEL FRAILICH

I Saw That!
Toronto

Published by I Saw That!, Toronto, Canada
http://isawthat.com

ISBN 978-0-9683347-5-1

CONTENTS

ACKNOWLEDGEMENTS

This book would not be possible without the help of many friends. First I would like to thank Mark Lewis for having pushed me, kicking and screaming, to dust off my old graphology skills and start doing readings, some twenty years ago. My experiences from that time are what motivated me to write this book.

Next, I would like to thank Dr. Mike Mandel, Thomas Baxter and Suzanne the Magician for their generous help and advice on some of the finer points of graphology, mentalism and the performance of close-up magic, respectively. I would also like to thank Tom Ransom, for sharing his knowledge of the history of mentalism; Ron Guttman, for being an early adopter; Steve Sharp, for his beautiful drawings for the trick 'Good advice'; and Alain Nu and Haim Goldenberg, for their enthusiasm and encouragement in the early stages of this endeavour.

I would like to thank my many local magician friends whose advice and suggestions helped turn a good manuscript into a much better one: Owen Anderson, Christina, James, Fernanda, Sammy, James, Lisa, Mark, Deborah, Mahdi, and all the rest—you know who you are!

Last but not least, I would like to thank Paul Pacific for being my sounding board at all hours of the day and night, for answering all my mentalism questions, no matter how trivial, with patience and enthusiasm, and for evaluating my mentalistic concoctions with the expert eye of a professional.

To all these people, I am greatly indebted.

Introduction

INTRODUCTION

If you've never done readings before—whether you're a magician or a mentalist—you're in for a treat. The moment you do the briefest of readings in your act, you'll instantly become more interesting as a performer and have greater rapport with your audience, especially with women. People will line up for readings after your show. If you do readings at work or in school, you'll meet new people and become more popular. If you offer readings at private or corporate events, you'll get more work and make more money. And all for the price of a few hours spent reading this book.

Readings provide something that magic or mentalism alone cannot. When you perform a magic trick or a mental experiment, it's about you, for the most part. You're the focal point and the centre of attention. There are ways to make magic and mentalism more about the spectator, but a reading is entirely about the spectator, and that makes it automatically more relevant and interesting to her. You're catering directly to the spectator's ego, which is much more compelling than any trick can ever be. People love to hear about themselves.

There once was a magician who was hired by a large company to entertain at a banquet. As he approached one table, a woman sitting there told him, in essence, to go bother some other table, because she and her friends were having a good time and didn't want to have it ruined by tricks. So he performed for another group. As usual, he ended his act with a short palm reading. He turned to leave—and there were three women lined up behind him to have their palms read… including the woman who had chased him away earlier! The magician was none other than Lee Earle who, partly due to this experience, turned to mentalism and readings and went on to become one of the biggest names in these fields[1].

Feeding the ego is so compelling that we do it to ourselves. Most of us think that we're better than others, or at least better than average, in some desirable way. This has been shown time and again in surveys and studies:

---

1   In his book, *The Classic Reading*.

- most people think they're less prejudiced than others in their community;
- most businesspeople think they're more ethical than their peers;
- most drivers think they're better drivers than average—even those who are in hospital after an automobile accident, and even when it's clearly their own fault!
- 60% of high school students think that they're in the top 10% of achievers;
- a staggering 94% of university professors believe that they are the better professors.

It's obviously very crowded at the top.

While a high opinion of oneself provides a good deal of ego satisfaction, flattery coming from another person can have an even stronger effect. And if that other person happens to be both a stranger and an expert, the effect is at its strongest. After all, an expert supposedly knows the truth, and a stranger is most likely to be impartial. Far be it from us to challenge these assumptions!

To provide an ego boost, you don't even have to hit the spectator's field of interest, nor do you have to reach for superlatives; you only have to say a few things that make her look good. With handwriting analysis, you do this by describing a character trait in a positive light. For example, if you see that a person is guided by emotions, you say: "*You follow your heart*" or "*You live life with passion*". As long as you come across as being sincere, even a little bit of flattery will get you everywhere. Make people feel good and they'll keep coming back for more.

So read on. Spend an evening studying the basics of handwriting analysis in the following chapter, and the next day, you'll be able to pick out a few positive traits and say something intelligent—and flattering!—about a spectator, just by looking at a few words written on a playing card or a billet. In a week or two, you can be ready to do full readings as an additional service you provide and increase your income, if you so desire.

Just try to resist the urge to claim that you're the top handwriting expert in the country.

Why handwriting analysis?

There is no shortage of reading systems. Psychic entertainers use, or pretend to use, astrology, numerology, Tarot cards, the I Ching, palmistry, and other systems for readings. So why consider yet another one?

Handwriting analysis, or graphology, is a method of character analysis based on psychological principles. This gives it a legitimacy denied to fortune-telling systems, since they belong to the realm of the supernatural. Although there are plenty of people who believe in the supernatural—and many who want to believe—there are also a lot of skeptics. But many skeptics who would ridicule any hint of the supernatural are willing to accept the validity of graphology with little or no hesitation.

This is at least partly due to media exposure. For example, many people now know that more and more corporations are using handwriting analysis to select job applicants and evaluate employees for promotion. Every so often, newspapers, even highly respected ones, publish graphological analyses of people who make the news, particularly in the case of presidential candidates during election years. Procedural police shows on television occasionally make use of a handwriting expert to help solve a case. Such things contribute to making graphology legitimate in the public's mind.

The fact that graphology has nothing to do with fortune-telling also makes it acceptable in situations in which the supernatural is not. Performers who are not comfortable with the idea of divination or the occult can thus do readings without compromising their principles, integrity or beliefs. For the same reason, graphology readings can be presented to audiences who would frown at any hint of the supernatural. According to Ty Kralin, a professional psychic entertainer, readers who do graphology are often more likely to get bookings than other readers, for precisely this reason[2].

Graphology has other advantages for the reader. There is no need to wrestle with the moral and ethical dilemmas involved in making predictions. There is no chance of being confronted, at a later date, by irate spectators complaining about unrealized predictions. There is no risk of different subjects finding out that they got exactly the same reading,

---

2   In his article in *Syzygy*, Quarterly Supplement #10.

or of the same subject getting different readings at different times, as can happen with systems based on stock (scripted) readings[3]. Finally, mistakes are easily explained away: the handwriting sample may be too small, a much more detailed—and therefore expensive—analysis may be required, and so on.

These reasons may well explain graphology's growing popularity with psychic entertainers. It has been used for decades already as a presentational device for cold readings. In recent years, more and more readers have been incorporating actual graphology into their readings. Today, there are even readers who use graphology exclusively.

Graphology also has the advantage of being easy to incorporate into a magic or mentalism performance. Any effect in which a spectator writes something down or signs a card provides an opportunity to deliver a brief reading. This is much less disruptive than other systems, which require additional actions to be taken to prepare for the reading, such as laying out cards, tossing coins, or examining a palm. Incidental readings add something unusual and interesting to a performance, enhance the performer's reputation, and advertize this additional skill, a hint that can lead to more work.

Last, but certainly not least, graphology is an extremely useful tool for mentalists. Perhaps the oldest application is the use of incidental readings to cover a discrepancy in Q & A procedure. Eddie Fields is often credited with being the first to use this approach. It was later popularized in Cicardi's "Psi-Grafico[4]", a routine—or whole act—that one could call a modern classic.

The most interesting and versatile use of graphology in mentalism is as a presentational device. In recent years, a new trend has emerged: mentalists are increasingly dropping the image of the mystic and replacing it with that of the expert in human behaviour. Performers like Derren Brown in the UK, Marc Salem and Banachek in the USA, and Thomas Baxter in Canada, to name a few, claim to use psychology and related disciplines, rather than psychic ability, to explain their feats.

---

3 To avoid these problems, such systems usually require the use of an additional system to remember what was said to whom.

4 Described in Bascom Jones' *Magick*.

Graphology, of course, fits perfectly into this modern style of presentation. In fact, its full potential may yet to be realized, at least according to Lee Earle. In his piece "Seven Success Secrets[5]", he recommends that all mentalists learn graphology: "*This will be the hot premise for a lot of future Mentalism because it bridges the gap between the believable and the impossible.*"

There can be no higher endorsement than that.

A note about this book

I'm a firm believer in non-sexist writing. Unfortunately, it often results in convoluted sentences, needless repetition, and grammatical ugliness, so I took the liberty of using a shortcut. Since the majority of magicians and mentalists are male, and the spectators most interested in readings—or at least willing to admit to it—are female, generally I use *he* to refer to the performer, and *she*, to the spectator, throughout this book[6]. I beg your indulgence.

---

5 In his book, *M.I.N.D.*

6 The actual ratio is about 30% men to 70% women, unless the readings are free (e.g., parties, corporate events), in which case it's a free-for-all.

Graphology

GRAPHOLOGY

WHAT EXACTLY IS GRAPHOLOGY?

If you were to observe a number of people doing physical tasks, you would find that there is a lot of variation in their motions. Some people move quickly, others take their time, still others are hesitant. Some people's motions are very precise, others are broad and sweeping. Some are fluid, others are strained or laborious. Some people have a delicate touch, others are heavy-handed. And so on.

The way in which we move says something about us. A person whose motions are forceful probably has a lot of drive, whereas a person with very soft gestures probably goes with the flow. A person who moves quickly probably makes decisions more quickly than a person who moves slowly.

Just as you can learn a lot about people by observing their gestures, you can learn much from their handwriting. A written piece is a record of a person's gestures; every motion leaves a trace. These traces can be interpreted as clearly as the gestures themselves. In fact, they provide much more information than gestures, because the act of writing involves many more parts of the brain than most activities. So much so, that handwriting analysis is also used as a medical tool to diagnose brain trauma.

Here's something you can try for yourself. From nothing more than a quick glance and without reading them, can you tell which sample was written by Harry Houdini and which by Prof. Einstein?

Chances are that the first thing you noticed about these two handwritings is the difference in size. From this, you may have concluded—

11

either consciously or subconsciously—that the larger one belongs to a showman, to someone who is "larger than life", and you would be right. A closer look at the smaller handwriting may have given you an impression of order and quiet intelligence, traits that fit an academic to the... letter.

When we first learn to write, we put a lot of conscious effort into forming the letters correctly. As time goes on and we write every day in school, the motions become automatic and unconscious; we no longer need to think about forming the letters. Slowly, our individual writing style emerges. It's an imprint of who we are; no two handwritings are ever completely alike. It's no wonder, then, that people throughout history have wondered whether there's any meaning to the various shapes and strokes of writing, and set out to study them.

SOME BACKGROUND YOU SHOULD KNOW

Modern graphology originated in 19th century France, from which it spread to many European countries. In the early 20th century, it was aligned with the principles of psychological character analysis. It uses much of that field's theory and vocabulary. Today, several systems of graphology exist, with different approaches and philosophies.

The popularity and acceptance of graphology varies by country. For example, in many parts of Europe, graphology is a highly respected branch of psychology, and in France, some 80% of companies use graphological analyses to screen job applicants. In the USA, graphology is considered a pseudo-science and only a few hundred companies use it. Graphology is also used for many other purposes besides employment screening: career counselling, business and marital compatibility, character analysis for self-knowledge, diagnosis of psychological problems and learning disabilities, jury screening, and medical diagnosis. Although there are some people who believe that handwriting can be used for fortune-telling, this notion is rejected by graphologists and, in fact, expressly prohibited by graphological associations.

A few definitions

The word *graphology* refers to the study of handwriting to determine character traits.

The analysis of handwriting and many other aspects of a document, in order to detect forgeries and establish authorship, is a forensic science that goes by several names, especially *forensic document analysis, questioned document examination,* and *handwriting examination.* Although forensic handwriting examination has virtually nothing to do with graphology and is of no interest for readings, it is a very valuable presentational device (e.g., for lie detection effects), and is thus worth a bit of study. Much information on this topic is available online.

Handwriting analysis can refer to either forensic or graphological analysis, but to avoid confusion, most people in these fields use it for graphology only.

Graphoanalysis is the name of a particular school of graphology. It is a registered trademark of the International Graphoanalysis Society.

Finally, graphologists use the word *handwriting* to refer to the sample itself: we talk about "the size of a handwriting", for example, rather than "the size of a person's handwriting".

GRAPHOLOGY FOR ENTERTAINMENT

If you were to go to a graphologist to have your handwriting analysed, he would ask for several samples of your writing, preferably spanning several years. He would spend some time looking at each sample, getting an overall impression of each one, looking for similarities, differences and patterns. Then he would go through the process of analysing every aspect of your writing, with the help of a magnifying glass, a ruler, a protractor and a non-writing point, and paint a psychological portrait that describes you, first in broad strokes, then in detail. You would get everything: the good and the bad, the pretty and the ugly, your strengths and weaknesses, what you want the world to see and what you want to keep hidden, and so forth. The whole process would have taken two to four hours.

Fascinating as such an analysis is, it's neither necessary nor desirable for our purposes. When you do a reading as part of a trick, you only make one or two brief statements that are either flattering or neutral, then continue with the trick. When you do a full reading, you make the person feel good about herself and move on to the next person as quickly as possible. Readings should thus be short and positive.

The graphology system described in this book is tailored specifically to these needs. It looks at a dozen signs that are easy to recognize and that have either neutral or positive interpretations. In addition, it's taught in a way that's easy to learn. It takes advantage of things you already know. You can learn the basic concepts in less than an hour and memorize the whole system in a few evenings. It's a good idea to collect as many samples of handwriting as you can find, from friends, family, colleagues and so on, and spend some time practicing. In no time, you'll be ready to do readings and, if you so choose, make a profit from your new skills.

THE BASICS OF HANDWRITING

We all learn to write by following a standardized model, called a *schoolbook model*. Over time, our handwriting evolves from the model until it becomes our own. It is therefore quite accurate to say that a graphological analysis consists, to a large extent, of finding and interpreting the differences between the handwriting and the model. It's worth spending a few minutes looking at a schoolbook model to remember what it looks like. Although there are variations across schoolbook models, they are minor enough that any model can be used as a starting point.

Below is a sample schoolbook model. In Western alphabets, almost every lower-case (or *small*) letter has a *body*. The body is the main part of the letter; in the illustration, it's the part between the dotted and solid lines. The letters 'a', 'c', 'e', 'i', 'm', 'n', 'o', 'r', 's', 'u', 'v', 'w' and 'x' have only a body. The letters 'b', 'd', 'h' and 'k' have a body and also a stem or a loop going upward, above the body, called the *ascender*. The letters 'g', 'j', 'p', 'q', 'y' and 'z' have a body and also a stem or a loop going downward, below the body, called the *descender*. The letters 'l', 'f' and 't' don't have a body; 'l' has an ascender, 'f' has both an ascender and a descender, and 't' has an ascender and a *bar*.

When combined to form words, letters are joined to each other with *connecting strokes*. In school, we are taught to join the final stroke of one letter to the initial stroke of the next letter, but as writing becomes second nature, we connect letters with a single stroke.

a b c d e f g h i j k
l m n o p q r s t u
v w x y z . ' ? " " !
A B C D E F G H I
J K L M N O P Q R
S T U V W X Y Z

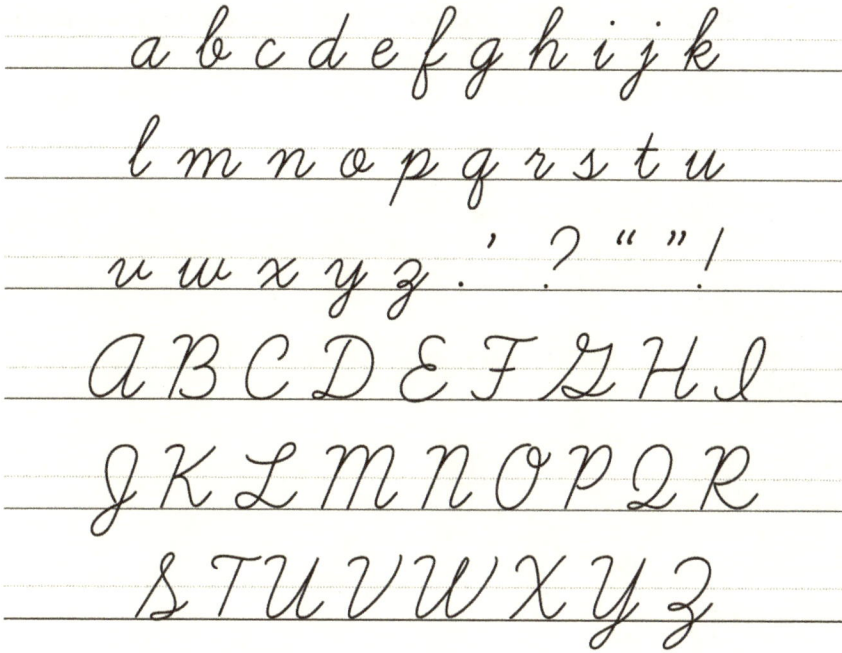

INTRODUCING THE SIGNS

If handwriting reflects our gestures, then it makes sense to relate it to body language. Indeed, many graphological signs are a reflection of a corresponding gesture. For example, to signal that we need space, we may spread our arms; in writing, this need is mirrored by wide spaces between words. The meaning of most signs can be easily interpreted in a similar way.

In this section, you will learn the meaning of the twelve signs that make up the system. Each sign is introduced with a question for you to answer before reading on. This will help you understand and remember the meaning of the signs better than if you just read the explanation. Chances are that your first impression will be right. When looking at the samples, assume that they're written on blank, unlined paper, which is preferred for graphological analyses.

For each sign, the graphological name of the sign and the trait it refers to are shown in **bold**. These names will be used throughout the rest of the book. The emphasis in this section is on the meaning and symbolism of each sign. Detailed explanations and all the possible variations are described in the next section.

Which writer is more sociable?

The quick brown fox jumps

The quick brown fox jumps

There are people who would love to be with others twenty-four hours a day, people who would love nothing more than to be left alone and live on a desert island, and people who are somewhere between these two extremes.

We can determine **sociability** from the **slant** of a handwriting. This is the angle of the up-and-down strokes, relative to the vertical. When we talk about relating to people, we talk about reaching out, about moving toward someone. Since we write from left to right, the rightward direction means forward and toward others, and the leftward direction means backward and toward the self.

The more a handwriting leans to the right, the more the writer moves toward others, and the more it leans to the left, the more withdrawn the writer is. The majority of people have writing that leans slightly to the right, which indicates normal sociability. Vertical writing means that the writer isn't particularly sociable, but not to the point of being reclusive.

Which writer looks to the future?

The quick brown fox jumps over the lazy dog. The quick brown fox jumps over the lazy dog. The quick brown fox jumps over the lazy dog. The quick brown fox jumps over the lazy dog. The quick brown fox jumps over the lazy dog. The quick brown fox jumps over the lazy dog.

Some people are strongly attached to their past. Other people can't wait for the future, looking forward to tomorrow with enthusiasm. In between are people who are not particularly pulled in either direction.

We can determine the writer's attitude toward the **past and future** from the left and right **margins** of a document. This is the blank space between the writing and the edges of the sheet. As time goes on, we go forward; we move away from the past and toward the future. The rightward direction means forward, therefore the future, and the leftward means backward, the past.

When the writing is toward the left, with a narrow left margin and a wide right margin, the writer is attached to the past. When the writing is toward the right, with a wide left margin and virtually no right margin, the writer welcomes the future. When there are clear margins on both sides of the text, the writer has a balanced attitude toward the past and the future.

Which writer needs more personal space ?

The quick brown fox jumps

The quick brown fox jumps

Some people like to be close to others and some people need space to themselves. This is independent of how sociable these people are; even the most people-loving person may feel crowded at times and want to pull back.

A person's need for **space** is seen in the **word spacing**, the space between words. If this space is wider than a wide letter, like 'm' or 'w', word spacing is wide. If it's narrower than a wide letter, word spacing is narrow.

Wide word spacing means that the writer needs space or may crave solitude. Narrow word spacing means that the writer is comfortable being close to others. Normal word spacing means the writer needs a normal amount of space.

Which writer is more upbeat?

The quick brown fox jumps

The quick brown fox jumps

Some people are generally optimistic and in a good mood, others are pessimistic, sometimes even gloomy. In between are people who aren't particularly pulled in either direction.

Mood is indicated by a handwriting's **baseline**. This is the line created by the bottom of the letter bodies. We associate the positive with the upward direction and the negative with the downward direction. We talk about feeling upbeat and about feeling down, about things looking up and about things that come crashing down. The direction of the baseline tells us the mood or attitude of the writer.

The future being to the right, a rising baseline means that the future looks positive, while a falling baseline means that it looks negative. This tells us whether the writer is optimistic and enthusiastic, or pessimistic and possibly discouraged. In between is the horizontal baseline, which means that the writer is calm, on an even keel, not particularly pulled either way by mood.

Which writer stands out in a crowd?

The quick brown fox jumps

The quick brown fox jumps

Some people command attention the moment they enter a room. They grab everybody's attention just by being themselves, effortlessly. They stand out. Then there are people who are invisible, so to speak, who go around unnoticed by most. In between are the majority of people: when they join a group, they blend in without particularly standing out.

Presence is indicated by the **size** of a handwriting. This is defined as the height of the letter bodies. We talk about people being larger than life or about feeling small and insignificant. The bigger something is, the more it gets noticed, and the smaller it is, the less attention it gets.

People with large writing stand out in a crowd, people with small writing are reserved and may wish to go unnoticed, and people with average-sized writing blend in easily.

Which writer likes to make an impression?

The quick brown fox jumps

The quick brown fox jumps

There are people who like to make a strong impression on everybody they meet. At the other extreme are people who are modest, who don't like to make a fuss about themselves. In between are people who are happy to present themselves as they are.

If the bodies of the letters represent our outer, public self, then capitals represent our inner, private self. Just like the height of the letter bodies shows how we appear to others, the height of the **capitals** show how we desire to appear, how much **recognition** we want.

Capitals that are disproportionally large for the body of the letters mean that the writer wants to make an impression, and small capitals, barely larger than the letter bodies, indicate modesty. Capitals that are in proportion to the size of the writing show that the writer is not particularly pulled in either direction.

Which writer has more drive?

The quick brown fox jumps

The quick brown fox jumps

Some people have so much physical and mental energy that they usually accomplish whatever they set out to do, and some people can only follow others because they don't have the energy to go against the current, so to speak. Most people are somewhere in between, accomplishing what needs to be done without too much trouble.

Our desire, ability and determination to accomplish things, our **drive**, can be gauged by the **pressure** of the pen on the paper. The amount of pressure we exert on the pen while writing reflects our overall energy.

The greater the pressure, the more drive the writer has, and the lighter the pressure, the less drive. Pressure can be seen by the width and the density—the 'blackness'—of the strokes, or sometimes by feeling the back of the paper.

Which writer is more logical?

The quick brown fox jumps

The quick brown fox jumps

Some people solve problems by thinking logically, stringing ideas together until they reach a conclusion. Other people are guided by intuition, analysing separate bits and pieces until a picture emerges. Many people use a combination of the two.

If we look at letters as individual thoughts, then connected letters means connected thoughts, therefore logical thinking. Spaces between letters means silence between thoughts, during which leaps of intuition can appear. A writer's style of **internal processing** is seen in the frequency of the connections, called the **connectedness** of a handwriting.

When virtually every letter in a word is connected to the next one, the writer thinks logically. When the letters are disconnected, the writer is intuitive. Often, letters are connected in groups of three or four, followed by a break. This shows a combination of logical thinking and intuition.

Which writer is friendlier?

The quick brown fox jumps

The quick brown fox jumps

We relate to others primarily either through our emotions or through our intellect. Here we look at the two emotional ways of relating.

Some people show their feelings when they deal with others. They're open and friendly. Other people prefer to keep their feelings to themselves. They're more cautious and reserved.

The way we relate to people, our **interaction** with others, can be seen in the shape of the **connections**—the strokes we use to connect letters to each other and the way we write the letters 'm' and 'n'. When these strokes are curved, when the writing has a rounded look, we relate to others through our emotions.

When the writing has the general shape of a **garland**, with 'm's and 'n's that look more like 'u's, with letters that are wide open at the top, the writer is open about his or her own feelings and responds to the feelings of others. When the writing looks like a series of **arcades** or arches, closed at the top and rather narrow, the writer is more closed to displays of feelings and more distant toward others.

Which writer speaks his mind?

The quick brown fox jumps

The quick brown fox jump

Here we look at the two intellectual ways of relating to others.

There are people who act according to their own beliefs. They have strong principles and ideas about how others should think and act. There are also people who act according to the beliefs and feelings of others. They're diplomatic and tell people what they want to hear.

When the connections and the strokes that make up the 'm's and 'n's are straight, the writing is said to be **angular**. It has sharp points and often has a sawtooth shape. Such writing belongs to people who interact with others according to their own principles and beliefs. They may have a sharpness about them, as seen in the sharp points in the writing.

When the letters are formed indistinctly and words look like pieces of thread, the writing is said to be **thready**. The writer can see the other person's point of view and is likely to agree with him or her.

Which writer sees the big picture?

The quick brown fox jumped

The quick brown fox jumped

Some people can look at a problem and immediately get a clear picture of the situation, while others have to examine every detail before they fully understand it. Most people are in the middle.

Clarity of thought is seen in the **simplicity** of a handwriting.

Handwriting that is very efficient, in which letterforms or connections have been simplified, is a sign of great clarity of thought. Writing that is needlessly complicated, ornate or retouched, shows great attention to detail. Writing in which letterforms are simple, neither simplified nor complicated, is a sign of practicality.

Which writer has more individuality?

The quick brown fox jumps

The quick brown fox jumps

Some people like to conform, to be like everyone else. Other people march to the beat of a different drummer; they see, think and act in their own, original way.

Individuality is seen in the **originality** of the letterforms.

The more the letterforms are similar to the schoolbook model, the more conforming the writer. The more original, unusual letterforms or connections a handwriting contains, the greater the writer's individuality.

Which writer is more idealistic?

The quick brown fox jumps

The quick brown fox jumps

Some people are motivated by ideas and ideals—things of the mind. Others are motivated by their emotions, their feelings. Still others are motivated by instincts, by their body, by the physical and material world.

Motivation is reflected in the **dominant zone**. In graphology, handwriting is divided into three layers, called *zones*. The *middle zone* is the area that contains the bodies of the letters. The *upper zone* is the area that contains everything that's written above the middle zone, namely the ascenders and the upper part of capital letters. The *lower zone* is the area that contains everything that's written below the middle zone, namely the descenders.

The three zones of a handwriting represent the three aspects of human beings: mind, emotions and body. Just like the brain is at the top, the heart is in the middle and the feet are on the ground, the upper zone represents the mind, the middle zone represents the emotions and the lower zone represents the physical world, which includes the body. In most handwritings, one zone is proportionally taller than the others. This zone is called the dominant zone.

When the upper zone dominates, the writer is motivated by the mind and ideals. When the middle zone dominates, the writer is motivated by emotions and the happenings of daily life. When the lower zone dominates, the writer is motivated by instincts and the physical world.

Summary: Table of signs

SIGN	MEANING	INTERPRETATION
Slant	Sociability	Right slant: *Sociable* Vertical: *Head over heart* Left slant: *Reserved*
Margins	Past and future	Narrow left: *Attached to past* Left & right equal: *Balanced* Narrow right: *Drawn to future*
Word spacing	Space	Narrow: *Needs little space* Average: *Normal* Wide: *Needs space*
Baseline	Mood	Horizontal: *Calm, even* Rising: *Optimism* Falling: *Pessimism* Variable: *Variable mood*
Size	Presence	Large: *Stands out* Average: *Blends in* Small: *Reserved*
Capitals	Recognition	Large: *Likes to be noticed* Average: *Confident* Small: *Modest*
Pressure	Drive	Heavy: *Driven* Medium: *Healthy* Light: *Accepting*
Connectedness	Internal processing	Connected: *Logical* Grouped: *Mixed* Disconnected: *Intuitive*

Connections	Interaction	Garland: *Friendly, responsive* Arcade: *Cautious, distant* Angular: *Firm, principled* Thready: *Diplomatic*
Simplicity	Clarity of thought	Simplified: *Big picture* Simple: *Practical* Complicated: *Detail-minded*
Originality	Individuality	Original: *Individual* Schoolbook model: *Conforming*
Dominant zone	Motivation	Upper: *Mind, intellect, ideals* Middle: *Emotions, daily life* Lower: *Instincts, body, physical and material world*

Exercise 1

For each of the signs below, answer the following questions:
- What does this sign represent?
- What are the variations for this sign? (e.g., large, medium, small)
- How is each variation interpreted?

o Pressure

o Slant

o Baseline

o Capitals

o Connectedness

o Originality

o Type of connections

o Dominant zone

o Size of the handwriting

o Word spacing

o Simplicity

o Margins

Exercise 2

For each of the samples on the following pages, answer these questions:

- Are the connections angular, thready, like garlands, like arcades?
  What does this mean?

- Is this writing slanted to the right, to the left, or vertical?
  What does this mean?

- Are the capitals large, small or average?
  What does this mean?

- Is this writing original or does it conform to the schoolbook model?
  What does this mean?

- Is the writing toward the left, the centre or the right of the page?
  What does this mean?

- Does the upper, middle or lower zone dominate in this writing?
  What does this mean?

- Are the letters in each word connected, disconnected or mixed?
  What does this mean?

- Is this writing large, average or small?
  What does this mean?

- Is the space between words wide, average or narrow?
  What does this mean?

- Is the baseline horizontal or does it rise or fall?
  What does this mean?

- Is this written with light, medium or heavy pressure?
  What does this mean?

- Is this writing simplified, simple or complicated?
  What does this mean?

When there are two images, the upper one shows a portion at actual size, the lower one is reduced to show the whole block of text and the edges of the sheet. You can use it to determine the margins and baseline.

Samples number 1 and 6 are written with a soft pencil; assume average pressure. If you're unsure about a sign, re-read the description and follow your instinct.

Sample 1

Imagine that I had a pack of cards; fifty two, all different and I take of those cards and place it face down on the table.

Imagine that I had a pack of cards; fifty two, all different and I take one of those cards and place it face down on the table.

Sample 2

I am here writing to find out
my writing tells Ariel about
personality. I have heard about
before and am very interested to
results. I wonder if the resul

I am here writing to find out what
my writing tells Ariel about my
personality. I have heard about this
before and am very interested to see the
results. I wonder if the results will
be biased because Ariel knows me. We
will see.
— Mahdi Gilbert

Sample 3

Mi nombre es Maria Fer
Zamorano y quiero ser
cuando sea grande, quiser
tener una familia, ser fe
Sin importar la felicidad

Mi nombre es Maria Fernanda
Zamorano y quiero ser maga
cuando sea grande, quiero
tener una familia, ser feliz,
Sin importar la felicidad de
los demas.

Sample 4

Frenn Deep neath the crypt
St Giles
Elanne a shrilest that
resaunded Fon milles
Said the Vilan, Good G

Frenn Deep neath the crypt of
St Giles
Elanne a shrilest that
resaunded Fon milles
Said the Vilan, Good Crselay
Its Brealsen lamaytell

Sample 5

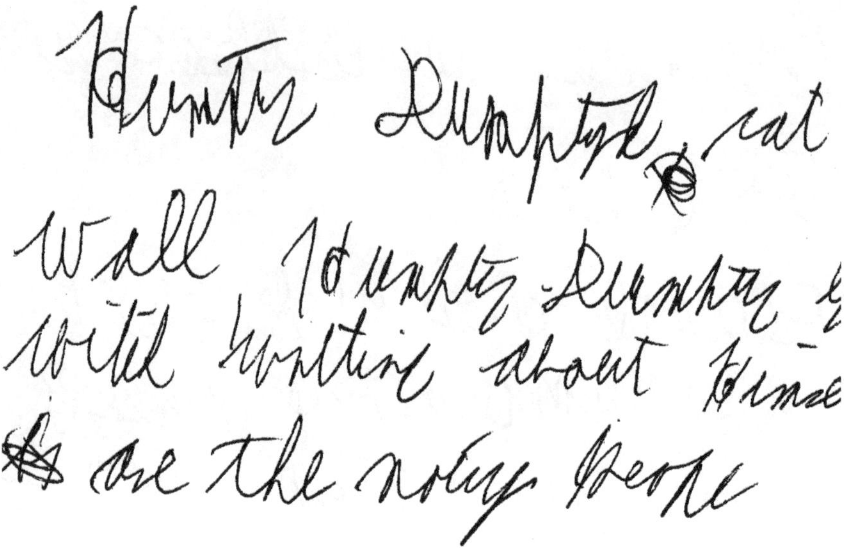

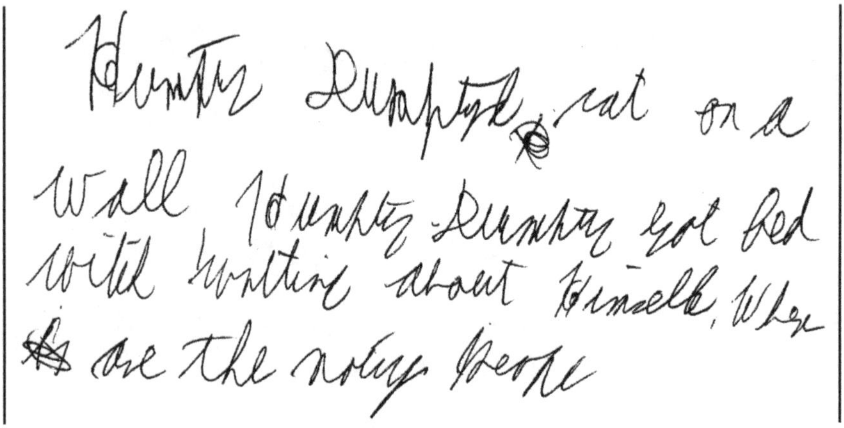

[handwritten text, first block:]

Humpty Dumpty sat
Wall Humpty Dumpty &
with writing about himse
are the noisy people

[handwritten text, second block (boxed):]

Humpty Dumpty sat on a
Wall Humpty Dumpty got fed
with writing about himself. When
are the noisy people

Sample 6

Sometimes its much easier and cheaper to
people think that something works ∧
than actually make it work.

Sometimes its much easier and cheaper to make
people think that something works rather
than actually make it work.

Sample 7

The bee is such a busy soul,
It has no time for birth cont
That's why in times like these
There are so many sons of bees

The bee is such a busy soul,
It has no time for birth control
That's why in times like these
There are so many sons of bees

Sample 8

Now is the time for all good men to come to the aid of the party of the first part.

Now is the time for all good men to come to the aid of the party of the first part.

Sample 9

Now is the time for all good
magicians to come to the aid
of their country.

Now is the time for all good
magicians to come to the aid
of their country.

Short samples 1

The following very short samples are typical of what you get on a billet or on the back of a business card. They are reproduced at actual size. Margins are of no significance here. Block printing is discussed later, but see what you can make of it before reading about it.

TH QUICK BROWN FOX

I went to the Lake today

There is magic in the air

You & I against the World.

There are tricks in all trades

Short samples 2

hi my name is Mike

Years of magic

My name is Paul

I reject the need for cursive

Magic is a means to mystify

Today, you finished reading about the basic concepts of graphology and practiced putting them to use. Tomorrow, when you look at someone's handwriting, you may remember that a right slant means 'sociable', and from that, work out that a left slant means 'reserved'. With nothing more than these two bits of information, you can already say something interesting about a person!

Collect handwriting samples from friends, colleagues and family, and analyze them to see what you can find out. Keep the samples and your results, as you'll be revisiting them after you learn more about the signs.

THE SIGNS IN DETAIL

Slant: Sociability

Description
The slant of a writing is the angle of the up- and down strokes. Writing can lean to the left, it can be vertical, it can lean to the right or the slant can vary within a line, sometimes even within a word. The amount by which the slant varies can be small—a few degrees—or it can be large, going from leaning strongly to the left, to leaning strongly to the right, with few or many steps in between.

Writing that leans up to five degrees from vertical is also considered vertical writing.

The quick brown fox jumps

The quick brown fox jumps -5° 0° +5° *t t t*

The quick brown fox jumps

The quick brown fox jumps

Interpretation
Most people are sociable. They enjoy interacting with people, they have empathy for the feelings of others, they like spending time with friends. Their writing leans to the right.

Some people don't particularly enjoy the company of others and prefer to be alone. They avoid emotional involvement and appear cool and reserved around others. They can be withdrawn, loners who would be happy to live on a desert island. Their handwriting leans to the left.

In between are people who don't mind interacting with others but aren't drawn to them. Their head rules over their heart. They make decisions based on reason rather than emotion. Their writing is vertical.

There are also people whose need and enjoyment of others varies. They can be warm and sociable at times, cool and withdrawn at others. This shows up as writing in which the slant varies.

Although most experts agree that the interpretation of right and left is as valid for left-handed writers as for right-handers, some authors claim that this is not always so. In very rare cases, a left slant may indicate sociability and a right slant may indicate introversion in the handwriting of a left-hander.

Margins: Past and future

Description

Margins are the amount of blank space between the edges of the sheet and the writing. In our system, we only look at the left and right margins.

If the block of text seems to be shifted toward the left edge of the page, or if the left margin becomes gradually wider or narrower as it goes down the page, we say that the left margin is narrow.

If the block of text is shifted toward the right edge of the page and the right margin is practically nonexistent, we say that the right margin is narrow.

If the left margin varies considerably, with some lines starting close to the left edge of the page and others much farther to the right, we have variable margins.

If there are obvious, straight margins on both sides, we say that the margins are balanced.

The quick brown fox jumps over the lazy dog. The quick brown fox jumps over the lazy dog. The quick brown fox jumps over the lazy dog. The quick brown fox jumps over the lazy dog. The quick brown fox jumps over the lazy dog. The quick brown fox jumps over the lazy dog.

The quick brown fox jumps over the lazy dog. The quick brown fox jumps over the lazy dog. The quick brown fox jumps over the lazy dog. The quick brown fox jumps over the lazy dog.

The quick brown fox jumps over the lazy dog. The quick brown fox jumps over the lazy dog. The quick brown fox jumps over the lazy dog. The quick brown fox jumps over the lazy dog. The quick brown fox jumps over the lazy dog.

Interpretation

Left and right, in addition to self and others, also has the symbolic meaning of past and present. For margins, we use the latter interpretation.

Some people are attached to the past and want nothing to do with the future. Their writing is shifted to the left of the sheet, with a narrow left margin and a wide right margin.

Some people are forever trying to move away from the past or are constantly being pulled back toward it. This shows up in the first case as a left margin that widens as it goes down the page, and in the second as a left margin that narrows down the page. In both these cases, the right margin is irrelevant, because the shifting nature of the left margin already indicates a movement toward—or away from—the future. In our system, we interpret all three cases above simply as 'attached to the past'.

Some people are drawn toward the future and away from the past. Their writing is shifted to the right of the sheet, with a noticeable left margin and a very narrow or nonexistent right margin.

Some people are constantly being drawn to one or the other. This is seen in an irregularly shaped left margin, with lines starting seemingly at random throughout the page.

Finally, some people have a balanced attitude toward past and future, with no particular attachment to either. Their writing is fairly centred on the page, with clear left and right margins.

Occasionally, you may come across a handwriting in which both the left and right margins are very narrow or even nonexistent. The interpretation of this sign has nothing to do with past and present, and therefore falls outside the scope of our system.

Word spacing: Need for space

Description

Word spacing is the average amount of space that the writer leaves be-tween words. Normally, this space is about the width of one of the wider letters, like 'm' or 'w'. This is average word spacing. If the amount of space is generally wider than a wide letter, then word spacing is said to be wide. If the space is consistently narrower than a wide letter, then the word spacing is said to be narrow.

The quick brown fox jumps

The quick brown fox jumps

The quick brown fox jumps

Interpretation

Some people can't get enough of other people. They never seem to tire of interacting with them. They write with narrow spacing between words.

At the other end are those who find it tiresome to deal with people. They can be very sociable and comfortable around others, but they feel crowded easily. They need a lot of space or time alone. They write with wide spacing between words.

In between are people who require a normal, healthy amount of space. They're capable of interacting with others for reasonable lengths of time and equally capable of spending time alone. They write with average word spacing.

Baseline: Mood

Description

The baseline refers to the shape and direction of the (often imaginary) line on which the body of the letters rest.

First, the baseline can be straight. In this case, it can be horizontal, it can rise steadily or it can fall steadily. There's also the case of the straight line that curves down at the right end; for our purposes, we consider this to be a horizontal straight line.

The quick brown fox jumps

The quick brown fox jumps

The quick brown fox jumps

The quick brown fox jumps

Second, the baseline can be curved. It can be concave, like a dome: rising, then falling. It can also be convex, like a bowl: falling, then rising.

The quick brown fox jumps

The quick brown fox jumps

Third, the baseline can be broken. Each word starts on the baseline but slants, either up or down.

The quick brown fox jumps

The quick brown fox jumps

And fourth, the baseline can be wavy. It can be smooth, undulating gently throughout the line, or it can be uneven, changing direction abruptly, often more than once.

The quick brown fox jumps

The quick brown fox jumps

Interpretation

A straight, horizontal baseline belongs to the person whose moods are in balance, who stays on course, working steadily to reach a goal.

For all other cases, we use the symbolism of upward being positive, meaning optimism or enthusiasm, and downward being negative, meaning pessimism or discouragement. When a straight baseline rises steadily, the writer is optimistic; when it falls steadily, the writer is pessimistic or worries.

A concave baseline shows initial enthusiasm followed by discouragement. The writer starts out optimistic but balks at arising difficulties. Such people are eager to start something new but may not always see it through.

A convex baseline shows initial reluctance followed by enthusiasm. The writer starts out resisting but, once the initial difficulties are overcome, feels encouraged to see the task through. Such people may find it hard to start something, but once they do, they finish it.

When every word rises individually from the baseline, the writer courageously keeps trying harder but may not achieve satisfactory re-

51

sults. When every word falls from the baseline, the writer is constantly fighting discouragement. Every step is a struggle.

A wavy, uneven baseline indicates that the writer's mood changes, optimistic and enthusiastic at times, pessimistic and discouraged at other times. But if the baseline waves gently and smoothly, it means that the writer is adaptable, continuously adjusting to the situation at hand without overreacting.

Size: Presence

Description
The size of a handwriting is measured by the height of the middle zone. In the schoolbook model, the bodies of letters are usually about 3 mm (1/8 inch) tall. This is average height. Large writing is anything taller than that, and small writing is anything smaller.

The quick brown fox jumps } 3 mm

Interpretation
Some people are always the centre of attention. They're the life of the party and stand out in a crowd. They make a big impression on others and their handwriting is large.

Other people are hardly visible. They work behind the scenes, letting others take centre stage and bask in the glory. They're happy to go unnoticed and their handwriting is small.

In between are people who simply like to mix, who are neither the centre of attention nor invisible in the background. Their writing is of average height.

Capitals: Recognition

Description
Capitals refers to the size of capital letters relative to the letter bodies. They can be proportional, large or small by comparison.

Normal capitals look right for the handwriting. They're usually a bit taller than the ascenders, not much. The rule of thumb is that they should be about twice the height of the body of the letters.

Large capitals can be huge, sometimes many times the height of the letter bodies and usually very wide as well.

Small capitals are barely the height of the ascenders or smaller. They may not even be taller than the letter bodies.

2x{ *The quick brown fox jumps* }x

2x{ *The quick brown fox jumps* }x

2x{ *The quick brown fox jumps* }x

Interpretation

Whereas the size of a handwriting tells us how much attention the writer gets, the size of the capitals tells us how much attention she wants, how important it is for her to make an impression on others.

Some people want everybody to know who they are. When they join a group, they soon tell everybody what they do, what they've accomplished—maybe even how much they earn!—and often dominate the conversation. Their writing has large capitals.

At the other extreme are people who like to stay out of the limelight. It's not that they're shy or anti-social; rather, they're modest and unassuming. This is the person who silently joined the conversation ten minutes ago but whom you just noticed now. Such people's handwriting has small capitals.

In between are people who don't particularly care about being noticed or unnoticed. They simply appear confident. When they join a group, they become a part of it; they speak when they have something to say and let others speak when they don't. Their writing has normal size capitals.

Pressure: Drive

Description

The pressure of a handwriting reflects how hard the writer pressed the pen against the paper while writing. Pressure can be light, medium or heavy.

The quick brown fox jumps

The quick brown fox jumps

The quick brown fox jumps

Normal pressure, which we call 'medium', implies a certain firmness in moving the pen across the paper. The strokes look substantial and dark enough on the paper to be easily seen.

Some people press so hard against the paper that you may be able to feel the ridge made by the pen on the back of the sheet. The strokes are as broad as the pen allows. This is heavy pressure.

There are people who write with so little pressure that the pen barely touches the paper. The strokes are thin and light, sometimes so light that they are broken or interrupted, as if the pen were skipping. This is light pressure.

the *the* *the*

The pressure and 'blackness' of a handwriting varies with the writing instrument. It's easiest to see with standard #2 or HB pencils and fountain pens, but easier to feel on the back of the sheet with a ballpoint pen. Markers vary in hardness, some roller ball pens are fairly consistent, hard pencils don't 'spread' and almost always leave an indentation, whereas soft pencils do the opposite. In any case, a standard, good quality ballpoint pen is the most practical instrument for our purposes. It's good enough to show what we need to see and people are comfortable using it.

Interpretation

Some people naturally have a lot of drive—a combination of physical and mental energy—that they can channel into accomplishing whatever they want to do. Such people are often very successful. They write with heavy pressure.

At the other end are people who have little drive for lack of energy. This can be natural, but it can also be from illness or from difficulties in life sapping their energy. It's difficult for them to realize their ambitions, so they tend to accept things as they are. They write with light pressure.

Most people have a healthy amount of drive. They have the energy to do their work and enough left over to enjoy other activities. They're often reasonably successful and they write with medium pressure.

Connectedness: Internal processing

Description

Connectedness is the degree to which the letters of a word are connected or disconnected from each other. If the letters are generally connected, the writing is said to be connected. The rule of thumb is that five or more letters must be connected in long words, and all the letters must be connected in shorter words.

If the letters are generally connected in groups of three or four letters, the writing is said to be grouped. Less than that, or if all the letters are separated, the writing is said to be disconnected.

The quick brown fox jumps

The quick brown fox jumps

The quick brown fox jumps

There are handwritings in which the connecting strokes are faint or invisible. This happens when the writer lifts the pen between letters. Sometimes, the very beginning or end of the connecting stroke can be seen, sometimes not. Since connectedness is about intent, invisible connections are interpreted exactly as if they were visible. It is therefore important to make the effort to find them in a handwriting that looks grouped or disconnected at first glance.

This is best done by tracing a few words, slowly and carefully, with a non-writing point and examining the writing with a magnifying glass. With a bit of practice, you'll feel the motion used to go from one letter to the next. You may find that it flows smoothly and naturally from letter to letter or, on the contrary, that it stops and starts sharply, abruptly, with distinct breaks and changes of direction.

If you find invisible connections, add them to whatever visible ones are present in each word and evaluate the result as described above.

Interpretation

Connected writing is a sign of logical thinking and deductive reasoning. One idea leads to the next until a conclusion is reached. This is the writing of the Sherlock Holmes, but also of the doer, the 'man of action'.

Disconnected writing is a sign of intuition and creativity. The writer stops after every thought to make room for a thought, a feeling, an idea, an insight to come to the surface. This is the writing of the poet and the thinker.

Grouped writing is like a mixture of connected and disconnected writing, allowing for both logic and intuition. This is the writing of someone who is well balanced between thought and action.

Connections: Interaction

Description

Connections are the strokes that tie one letter to the next one. We look at the shape of the connections, but also at the shape of the letters in general and of the letters 'm' and 'n' in particular.

Overall, a handwriting can be rounded, angular or thready. In rounded writing, most strokes are curves, whereas in angular writing, most strokes are straight, or nearly straight, lines. In thready writing, many strokes look like squiggles.

When rounded writing looks like a row of cups or bowls strung together, open at the top like the letter 'u', and often fairly wide, we have garland connections. When it looks like a row of domes or arches, closed at the top like the schoolbook model of the letters 'm' and 'n', and often fairly narrow, we have arcade connections.

Angular writing has a zigzag or sawtooth shape. The points can be very sharp or somewhat rounded, but the rounded points don't change the overall shape.

In thready writing, the inner or final letters of words look like a piece of thread, a squiggle, a twisting curve, a wavy line.

Interpretation

We each have one primary way in which we relate to others.

People who are open with their emotions are friendly and open. Their writing is open at the top, shaped like a garland. Imagine extending your arms to hug someone: from your vantage point, your arms and chest form a 'u'.

People who prefer to keep their emotions private are cautious and reserved toward others. Their writing is closed at the top, in the shape of arcades. Imagine putting your arms over your head for protection: your arms form an arch, an arcade.

People who deal with others according to their own principles and beliefs don't respond to emotions. They're firm and may even be aggressive when dealing with people who don't share their views. They may 'bite'; their writing is in the shape of teeth, pointy, angular.

People who respond to the beliefs of others tell them what they want to hear. They're diplomatic. Their writing is thready. Think of the curves in the thread: the writer is constantly changing direction, following the thoughts of others.

Simplicity: Clarity of thought

Description
The simplicity of a handwriting is determined by whether the letterforms are simpler, similar to, or more elaborate than the schoolbook model.

If you were to trace a sample of handwriting with a smooth, non-writing point, you may find that the letters are formed in essentially the same way as the school model. The size, the proportions and the slant may be different, loops may be taller or wider, letters may be narrower or broader, strokes may be shorter or longer, straighter or more curved, and so on, but the letterforms are just a variation on the model, the motions used to form them are essentially the same. Imagine the schoolbook model being written on a sheet of rubber; if you stretch it or pull it in any or several directions at the same time, the writing will be distorted, but the essence of the letterforms remain. This is simple handwriting, writing in which every letter has roughly the same number of strokes as in the school model, and letters that are formed in roughly the same way.

In another sample, you may find that certain strokes have been simplified, others have been entirely eliminated, two or more strokes are combined into a single, simpler stroke, sometimes letters are connected in unusual but efficient ways. If you were to trace such a handwriting, you would find that it feels very different from writing according to the schoolbook model. There are fewer strokes and the letters are formed differently. The writing is very efficient; it has a great economy of motion. This is simplified handwriting, in which strokes are kept to a minimum and letterforms are reduced to their essence.

At the other extreme is writing in which there are unnecessary strokes or strokes that are more elaborate than they to need be. Here we find unusually complicated letterforms, fancy strokes in endings, extra loops inside letters, ascenders or descenders formed by several strokes or loops, strokes that extend into a zone they don't belong in, and so on. This is complicated handwriting.

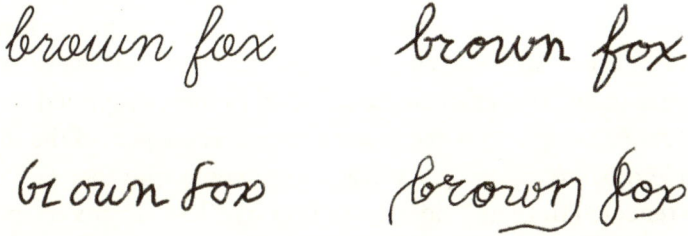

brown fox   *brown fox*

brown fox   *brown fox*

It's worth noting that schoolbook models from different countries (or eras) can be quite elaborate, such as the very fancy (contemporary) French model shown below. Typically, though, only the capitals are elaborate in these models, so focusing on the lower-case letters ensures that it is not mistaken for complicated handwriting.

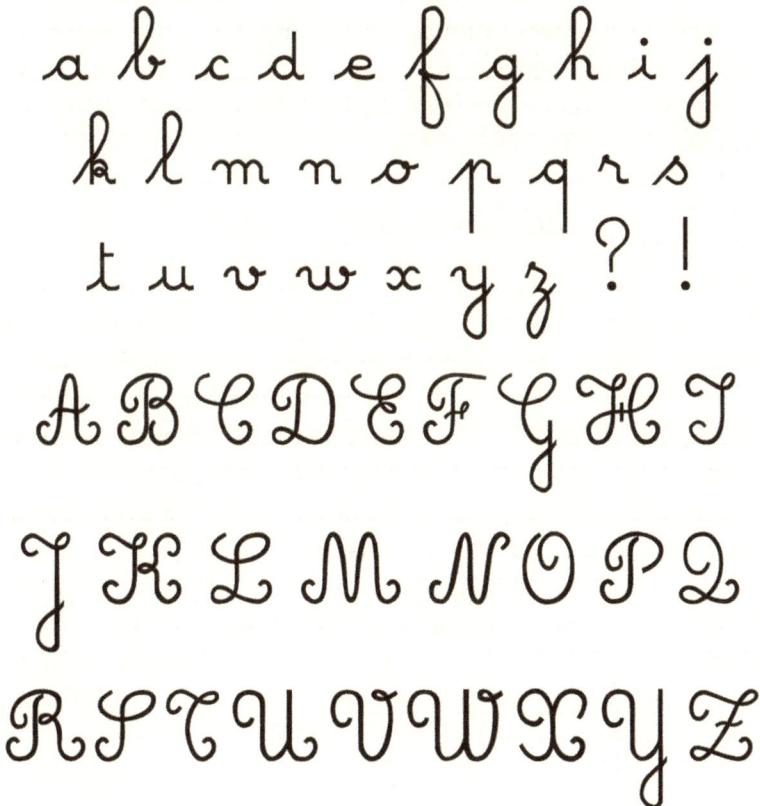

*a b c d e f g h i j
k l m n o p q r s
t u v w x y z ? !*

*A B C D E F G H I
J K L M N O P Q
R S T U V W X Y Z*

Interpretation

People who see the big picture are people who have cleared away all the unimportant details so that they can focus on the main points. Having fewer things to think about, they see the situation more clearly and can thus concentrate more efficiently and effectively on the situation or problem at hand. This efficiency is reflected in their simplified writing.

Conversely, people who need to examine every aspect of the situation or problem before making a decision are people who focus on details. This is reflected in their tendency to 'improve' letterforms according to some internal impulse, hence the complicated shapes and extra strokes of complicated writing.

People whose writing is simple—neither simplified nor complicated—strike a balance. They see enough detail so as not to lose track of the big picture, and enough of the big picture so as not to get lost in details. They deal with situations and problems in practical ways.

No one type is better than another. Each one is better suited to certain activities than to others. For example, the detail-minded person would make a good bookkeeper or mechanic, the big-picture thinker would make a good executive, and the practical person would make a good project manager or troubleshooter.

Originality: Individuality

Description

The originality of a handwriting is the degree to which there are letterforms that differ from the schoolbook model. A handwriting can look virtually identical to the model or it can be entirely different from it.

Writing that looks essentially like schoolbook writing, with only minor variations in size, proportion, slant, and so on, as described under Simplicity, above, is conventional writing. If there are letterforms or connections that are clearly different from the model, that are formed in a different way, with different strokes, then the writing is original. The more such letterforms exist in a handwriting, the more original it is.

The differences don't have to be dramatic; even small or subtle variations in strokes and letterforms are enough to classify a handwriting as being original (e.g., the 'm' and the 's' in 'jumps', below).

It's important to remember that simplified writing, by definition, is also original.

The quick brown fox jumps

The quick brown fox jumps

Interpretation

Some people have no interest or desire to stand out in any way. They like to fit in, to be like everybody else. They have conventional tastes and prefer to conform to the majority, to the standard. This is reflected in conventional handwriting.

Every departure from the schoolbook model is a sign of individuality. The greater the number of original letterforms or connections, the more individuality the writer possesses. Most people have some degree of originality in their handwriting.

Dominant Zone: Motivation

Description

Handwriting is divided into three zones: the middle zone, which extends from the top to the bottom of the letter bodies; the upper zone, which contains everything above the middle zone, namely the ascenders and the upper part of capital letters; and the lower zone, which contains everything below the middle zone, namely the descenders.

In schoolbook models, the three zones are roughly the same height, but over time, we tend to favour one zone over the others and it becomes taller than the other two. This tallest zone is the dominant zone. If the ascenders and the tops of the capitals are taller than the other parts, the upper zone is dominant. If the bodies of the letters are tallest, the middle zone is the dominant zone. If the descenders are tallest, then the lower zone is dominant.

Although most handwritings have one dominant zones, sometimes two zones are the same height, the third one being shorter (in the bottom example of the illustration below, the upper and lower zones are the same height, the middle zone is shorter). Then we have two dominant zones. There are also handwritings in which all three zones are the same height, in which case the three zones are in balance. These are very rare.

The quick brown fox jumps

The quick brown fox jumps

The quick brown fox jumps

The quick brown fox jumps

Interpretation

The mind is the source of beliefs, of thought, of imagination. It's about intellectual thought and abstract thinking, about dreams and ambitions, about vision, goals and ideals. A person motivated by the mind wants to accomplish things, realize dreams. The upper zone is dominant.

Emotions are more about the here-and-now. They come up in response to events, situations, experiences. A person motivated by emotions gets satisfaction from the moment and focuses on day-to-day concerns: interacting with people, work, home, family, everyday responsibilities, and so on. The middle zone is dominant.

Instincts are primarily about physical sensations and the body's interaction with the environment. A person motivated by instincts wants to fulfill the needs of the body and is interested in the physical and material world: food, sports, building things, business, money, and so on. The lower zone is dominant.

When two zones are dominant, it simply means that the writer is equally motivated by both realms, and when all three are equal, the writer is balanced between the three.

Congratulations! You've just finished learning all you need to know about the meaning of graphological signs and symbolism.

As you saw, graphology is easy to understand. More than anything else, it requires practice to learn to recognize the signs. Some, like slant, are very obvious, even to the rank beginner, while others, like originality, can be challenging to determine at first. Spend some time practicing on as many handwriting samples as you can find, and soon it will become second nature to you.

It's very important to remember that the traits found in a handwriting aren't necessarily reflected in the writer's behaviour. As you study the samples you've collected from friends, colleagues and relatives, you may be surprised to find, for example, that a certain person who doesn't interact much with people writes with a strong right slant, indicating sociability. This person may be shy or inhibited in some way, and therefore minimizes contact with others.

Conversely, you may find a warm, friendly and outgoing person whose writing is vertical. This person may have learned to behave more sociably, for whatever reason; it's also possible that she is emotional (dominant middle zone), genuinely empathetic, and communicative, but is just as happy being on her own as in the company of others.

There are all kinds of seemingly contradictory combinations, from the introvert who loves to stand out to the extrovert with a sharp tongue. Usually, when you tell people about such traits during a reading, they'll know exactly what you're talking about (and will often be impressed at your insight). For example, when you tell the shy introvert that she's a people-person, you can be sure that she knows that she's drawn to people but that something prevents her from interacting with them, since she probably faces that problem every day of her life.

At other times, you may face a blank stare, incomprehension, or even an accusation of being wrong. This happens when the person is not aware of the trait, either because it has never been an issue, or simply because she never gave it much thought. Thus, for example, an outgoing person with vertical writing may not be aware that she likes solitude as much as interaction, perhaps because she's always had to look after a large family and thus never had time for herself or, on the contrary, because she's been alone most of her life. In such cases, you may have to give a brief explanation of your findings. Expressions such as 'deep down' and 'a part of you' can come in handy. Once she understands, she may recognize the trait or thank you for giving her some insight about herself—or she may continue to disagree, in which case you can use one of the bits given under 'Challenges', in a later section of this book.

THREE SPECIAL CASES

Signatures

There are times when a signature is the only piece of writing available to us. In fact, sometimes it's the only logical thing to ask for, or the most practical to work with. We may ask a spectator to sign a card for a trick like the 'Card to wallet'; we may ask people to sign the back of a business card when doing short readings in a mentalism routine; we may ask a spectator for a signature when working a booth at a trade show. It's therefore useful to be able to analyse them.

The text we write is meant for others, so it reflects the way we appear to the world and how we deal with it. The signature is strictly about us, so it reflects our inner self. The meaning of a few signs therefore differ somewhat from the same signs in the text.

The baseline of a signature reflects the writer's desires. If it rises, it means that the writer has ambitions. If it falls, it means that the writer accepts things the way they are. A horizontal baseline has the same meaning as for text writing.

The initial capitals of the first and last names are compared to each other, not to the rest of the signature. Middle initials are ignored. If the initial of the first name is larger than that of the family name, the writer is a self-made man or woman. If it's the opposite, the writer credits his or her family, and if the two are equal, the writer's success comes from a combination of both. In the case of a woman signing with her married name, the same relationships hold with respect to her husband, rather than her family of origin. Below are the signatures of the ten most recent First Ladies of the USA. It's interesting to note how they almost all see themselves as equals to their husbands.

The margins, word spacing and size of a signature are of no interest to us. The remaining signs can be analysed and interpreted in the usual way. The slant, pressure, connectedness, connections, simplicity, originality and dominant zone thus have the same meaning as in text.

When a signature is nothing more than a squiggle—which is quite common—the best you can do is to do the best you can do! You will always be able to determine the pressure; if that's the only thing you can make out, then so be it.

Printing

Graphology works best on cursive writing—also called *connected* or longhand writing—but that's not always what we get. When spectators are asked to sign a card, they often print their name, sometimes in block letters. This also happens when writing on billets or what have you in the course of a mentalism performance. When doing one-on-one readings, you can ask the person to write in longhand, but even here, there is no guarantee, since many people write in printing style normally. To make matters worse, in recent years, some schools have stopped teaching cursive writing altogether.

brown fox   brown fox   BROWN FOX

Fortunately, it's not too hard to deal with printing. Most of the signs are still there and can be interpreted in the same way as for cursive writing. There are only a few points that differ.

In block lettering, all the letters are the same height. There are no capitals as such—they're all capitals—and there's no lower zone. However, it's easy to determine the height of the upper and middle zones. Look at the letters that are divided horizontally: the bar of the A and the H, the point at which the loops of the B, R and P join the stem, where the arms of the K meet each other or the stem, and so on. The distance from the division to the top of the letter is the equivalent of the upper zone, and from the division to the baseline is the equivalent of the middle zone.

If you have any experience in dealing with people or in doing readings, chances are that you can guess the relative height of the lower zone too. For example, if the writer is obviously a very physical person and the upper and middle zones are about equal, it's more likely that the lower zone is dominant, rather than all three zones being in balance. This is also likely to be the case for a businessperson or a real estate salesperson, since these occupations are strongly related to the material world (money, construction). You can always ask what the person does for a living. Since you're analysing handwriting and not claiming to be a psychic, it's perfectly acceptable for you to ask questions.

In all styles of printing, the connections are missing. But all is not lost: if you examine the writing carefully, chances are that you'll find clues to the missing parts. Although it's not too hard to learn a different style of handwriting, it's very difficult to change the way in which we draw strokes and stroke formations. They're very much part of who we are and therefore difficult to hide or disguise.

Look closely and you'll see whether the strokes tend to be curved or straight; look a bit more and you may well see the garland or the arcade shape coming up time and again. Or, on the contrary, you may find nothing but straight, hard lines with sharp points. You may find the beginning of a connecting stroke, or some of the stroke may actually be present but so faint that it's nearly invisible.

You can often get a good idea of the connections and connectedness of a writing—and other things as well—by tracing a few words of the sample with a non-writing point. This can be anything with a dull point that doesn't write and that won't damage the writing or the paper, like a stylus for hand-held computers, a clean, dried-out ballpoint pen, a short knitting needle with the end dulled with sandpaper and polished, a wooden burnishing tool used by graphic designers and artists, and so on. Follow the strokes carefully, as if you were trying to learn to write the same way, and soon you'll be able to feel the speed at which the writer wrote, the motion leading from one letter to the next, and much more. With practice, you can often deduce the missing information.

Foreign alphabets and scripts

You may well come across a sample written in a different language, for instance if someone asks you to look at the writing of a friend or relative. Foreign-language text can be analysed according to the principles described here, as long as the language uses some version of a Western-style alphabet (e.g., Slavic languages, Greek, even Vietnamese) and you ignore anything that has to do with specific letterforms, since many languages have their own unique letters. Of course, if you have learned that language and know its alphabet well, then you'll know what to take into consideration and what to ignore.

Below is a sample of handwriting of Russian writer Leo Tolstoy, the author of *War and Peace*. You can clearly determine the slant, word spacing, baseline, capitals, pressure, connectedness, and dominant zone. Connections require a bit more care, because you cannot look at the shape of the 'm's and 'n's, which are different letterforms in Russian, and you cannot say anything about simplicity and originality (and if you were looking at the original, you would, of course, also be able to determine size and margins).

For non-Western alphabets, it's best to simply admit defeat, rather than risk making wrong assumptions about the meaning of signs we take for granted in Western scripts.

HOW TO DO AN ANALYSIS

Tools

Professional graphologists use tools to help guarantee accuracy. These include a non-writing point for tracing, as described above, a magnifying glass, a pencil, a ruler, and a protractor. It's entirely up to you whether to use tools during an analysis or not. However, while learning, it's a good idea to use them to confirm your evaluation of the appropriate signs. For example, a baseline may look perfectly straight, but when checked with the ruler, you may find it to be slightly wavy.

If you decide to use a magnifying glass, you can use any model you like, but there's one style that's particularly worth mentioning. This is the folding, pocket magnifier made of three hinged pieces. It opens up in a 'U' shape. Most models have a measuring scale etched into the base, making it easy to measure writing size and zone heights.

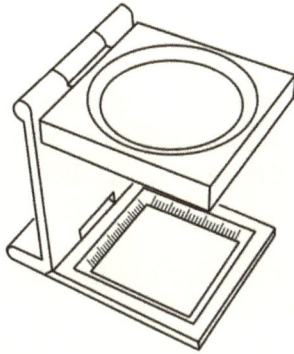

Analysing the signs

In a professional graphological analysis, there is a sequence of steps to follow. First, a basic picture is formed by looking at the page as a whole. Next, every sign is analysed, in order from most important to least important, and the picture is adjusted and refined accordingly. Finally, the findings are synthesized into a report, which is a full psychological profile of the writer.

Readings are much simpler. We look at the signs individually, without relating them to each other, and the meaning of each sign goes straight to the final report, which is simply a list of traits. There is no hierarchy and no synthesis, so there is no particular sequence to follow.

We can look at the signs in any order we choose, and jot down the traits as we find them. This gives us the freedom to create a sequence for the convenience of the analysis. Feel free to create your own. It could be based on viewing distance, use of tools, your visual acuity, personal preferences, or anything that makes it easier for you.

Slant

The slant is very easy to see, but it's not easy to determine whether a tiny right slant should be categorized as vertical or slanted to the right. With practice, you may be able to learn to recognize a 5° slant, otherwise you can measure the angle with the protractor.

Position the ruler as described above and draw a line across the baseline. Then find a typical vertical stroke, align the ruler with it and draw a line over it. The line should cross the baseline and extend the stroke by a good 8–10 cm (3–4 in) upward. Now take the protractor, align it with the baseline you drew and centre it where the extended stroke intersects the baseline. You can now measure the slant of the vertical stroke. Assuming that 0° is at the left and 180° is at the right, anything between 85° and 95° is determined to be a vertical slant.

Margins
The margins are visible at any distance, from arm's length to up close.

Word spacing
Chances are that you can determine the word spacing by close visual inspection alone. If not, measure the width of a typical wide letter and a typical space, or several of each and average them.

Baseline
The best way to evaluate the baseline is to scan the lines while holding the sheet perfectly straight at arm's length. In case of doubt, you can check with the ruler. Align it with the bottom of the first and last characters of a long line, then scan to determine the shape of the baseline and, if it's straight, its direction. Do this for several lines and determine the most common shape and direction.

Size and Capitals
With a bit of practice, you'll have no trouble determining the size of the capitals relative to the size of the writing. Determining the latter, however, takes a bit more practice and some estimation skill. In any case, you can measure both as described for the zones, below.

Pressure
Strong pressure may be visible at normal reading distance. If not, look at the writing carefully up close, using the magnifying glass if necessary.

Connectedness
If the connectedness isn't immediately obvious, examine the writing with the magnifier and, if necessary, trace a few words to determine if there are invisible connections, as described in the previous section.

Connections

The shape of the connections is easy to see at normal reading distance and up close.

Simplicity and originality

As you examine the writing carefully to find original letterforms and connections, you'll notice whether they're also simplified or not. In case of doubt, you can trace such letters with the non-writing point to find out if they're written with fewer strokes than is customary. With a bit of experience, however, you'll soon be able to recognize simplified writing without tracing.

Dominant zone

If one zone doesn't stand out, either at normal reading distance or up close, you can measure the height of all three zones. Pick a portion of a line where the baseline is more or less straight and draw four lines with pencil and ruler, making sure they're parallel: one across the top of the writing (top of the ascenders and/or capitals), one across the top of the letter bodies, one across the baseline, and one across the bottom of the descenders. Turn the sheet 90° and measure the height of each zone.

Is it or isn't it?

Many graphological signs are easy to recognize. The slant is constant and in one direction, or it varies. The text is to the left, to the right, or centred on the page. The baseline is straight or curved or wavy, and so on. But not all signs are as cut and dry as these. People aren't machines; gestures vary and so can handwriting. Word spacing may be uneven; some capitals may be unusually tall while others are average; one 'd' is clearly original in its stroke formation, but the others aren't; and so on. Such problems are particularly perplexing for the beginning graphologist. Where do you draw the line?

The important thing to remember is that we're looking for patterns. One instance—or even several—of something different doesn't necessarily change the pattern. Let's say that you're a good typist. You type accurately and rarely make mistakes. But being a good typist doesn't mean that you *never* make a mistake. Nor does making an occasional mistake mean that you're not a good typist. What's important is the pattern, not the exception.

Professional graphologists may see certain signs as being important under certain circumstances, even if they appear only once or twice in a document, but that's generally not the case for our purposes. Usually you can simply ignore the exceptions. If you want to put a number on it, ignore anything that occurs less than 20% of the time. If it's any more than that, then consider giving a split evaluation. For example, if half the capitals are large and half are average size, then evaluate the writer as varying between appearing confident and liking to be noticed.

There's nothing unusual or contradictory about such an assessment. We may feel confident about who we are when we're in one group, but would like to be noticed in a different group; for example, family and work. Many signs can be evaluated in the same way.

Finally, don't be afraid to use your own judgement and experience. It's a central part of graphology—and of readings—anyway.

Exercise 3

Repeat exercises 1 and 2 with your deeper knowledge of the signs. It's a good idea to follow all the advice given above, including the use of tools.

Readings

READINGS

THE INCIDENTAL READING

When performing magic or mentalism, you can do a very brief reading, no more than one or two points, to establish yourself as a handwriting expert. Saying something positive about the signs is not difficult; finding the one or two signs with which to do the reading, however, may prove to be a challenge. When doing full readings, you have several lines of text of a person's natural, unconstrained writing on a full sheet of paper to analyse. But in magic and mentalism performances, you don't have that luxury.

A spectator signs the face of a playing card, scribbles a word or two inside a drawing of a crystal ball in preparation for a centre tear, hastily writes something on a business card or a billet. The spectator is under pressure to hurry up so as not to slow down the performance. The writing often has to be done in the hands or the lap, for lack of a table, and with little elbow room available. These are hardly natural and unconstrained conditions. The writing may well be distorted in one or several ways, which makes the analysis unreliable.

This is particularly true in magic. In mentalism experiments, it's common to have several people write something, which reduces the pressure, and it's often possible to hand out a notepad or a stack of cards, for example, which provides some support for writing. This gives you a better chance of getting good samples. But in magic, usually you only have one sample: a signed card. Often, it's not even a signature but a scribble, or even a mere scratch of the pen. And it's written with a broad-tipped marker, for visibility, which makes analysis even more difficult.

If visibility is not an issue, there are several things you can do to increase your chances of getting a better sample: give the spectator plenty of time—"While you're doing that, I will…"—provide a writing surface, a pen or marker with a normal barrel—not a thick one—and a thin or medium tip. For mentalism, this is all you need to do; for magic, there are a few tricks in the Magic section that are geared specifically to getting good samples.

Once you have a sample in hand, look at it as a whole for a moment. If something stands out, use it to do the reading. Otherwise, you can almost always determine at least the slant and the size, sometimes the capitals or the dominant zone. These give you quite a bit already; even just being able to say: *"You're a people person"* or *"You're modest and keep to yourself"* can make quite an impression. It's best, of course, to say something that isn't immediately obvious; for example, telling a gregarious spectator that she's a people-person is not terribly impressive. However, telling the same spectator that she's just as happy being alone as with company is quite startling.

In the worst case, when you have nothing more than a scribble, just move on. You're the only one who knows what you were going to do, so the audience won't be any the wiser. If you have more than one trick in your act that involves writing, maybe you'll have more luck the next time.

Since an incidental reading is intended to be an aside to the main trick, you wouldn't want to use the tools, but if it suits your style, you can whip out the magnifying glass to study the writing for a moment before commenting on it. This lends you an air of authority, and if you like, you can make it into a gag with a humorous line, or even incorporate the magnifier into the trick.

Sample lines

Here are some sample lines tailored to incidental readings. They're all positive, brief, fairly broad and reasonably entertaining. If a trait is not listed, it's because it's not likely to be found in the sample, or there's nothing positive or interesting to say about it in a performance. For variety, or if you're not sure about a sign, you can phrase the statement as a question, e.g.: *"You're a bit of a loner, aren't you?"*. You can always add a knowing *"I thought so"* afterward.

Slant
When asked to sign a card, people often write at an angle, so use the baseline to determine the slant, not the edges of the card.
Right: *"You're a people person. You like to be around others."*
Vertical: *"Your head rules over your heart."*
Left: *"You may be a bit of a lone wolf."*
Variable: *"You like to be around people—but not all the time."*

Baseline
Only applies when not intentionally writing on an angle.
Rising: *"You're an optimist."*
Horizontal: *"You're not easily distracted. You stay on course."*

Size
Large: *"You get noticed. You're the life of the party."*
Average: *"You like to be around your peers."*
Small: *"You're more of a listener than a talker."*

Capitals
Large: *"You have a strong sense of your identity."*
Average: *"You're happy being who you are."*
Small: *"You're modest; there's more to you than people generally realize."*

Pressure
Heavy: *"You accomplish a lot."*
Light: *"You take things as they come."*

Connectedness
Connected: *"You're a logical thinker."*
Disconnected: *"You're very intuitive."*
Mixed: *"You're both logical and intuitive."*

Connections
Garlands: *"You're a friendly person."*
Arcades: *"You tend to be reserved around others."*
Angular: *"You have strong principles and beliefs."*
Thready: *"You're diplomatic."*

Simplicity
Simplified: *"You're an efficient thinker."*
Simple: *"You're a practical person. You get things done."*
Complicated: *"You're very precise. You pay attention to details."*

Originality
Original: *"You're a creative thinker."*
Conforming: *"You like to belong. You'd rather go with the flow than stand out."*

Dominant zone

Upper: *"You have high ideals or ambitions."*
Middle: *"You have a passion for living."*
Lower: *"You are down to earth."* You can add to this by asking whether the spectator is involved in food, business, sports, construction or manufacturing, according to whatever you can glean from the person's dress and appearance.

Block letters

"You like structure and you like to work with your hands." This is often the case for people who choose block letters over other kinds of printing. They're often involved in some technical field.

Of course, there's nothing to prevent you from bluffing a little bit. Since you usually know, either ostensibly or secretly, the identity of the writer, you can deduce a few things from the person's body language, behaviour, facial expressions, clothing and so on, and use that knowledge in conjunction with the graphological signs for your quick reading. Alternatively, you can learn a bit about cold reading, if you don't know it already, and use some information gleaned that way, or even use a stock line or two.

THE FULL READING

Writing materials

The paper should be good quality writing paper, standard size (letter or A4), blank, unlined and preferably white. It's very important to use unlined paper, because many people adapt the size of their writing to fit on the printed lines and respect the printed left margin. This invalidates any analysis of margins, size of writing and size of capitals.

You can use a writing pad or a few sheets held in a clipboard. The clipboard has the advantage of making it possible to write on the lap or at the edge of a table, if conditions aren't quite perfect, which happens occasionally. Portfolios and pad holders, made of leather or some other material, may look like they can do the same job as a clipboard, but in fact, most of them hinder the act of writing in some way. To be usable for our purposes, a holder has to be rigid, it has to lie flat on the table when the front flap is folded back to accommodate a left-handed writer, without any slack and without creating bumps in the writing surface, and without the closure, if there is one, curling up over the paper. Very few holders meet all these conditions. You can always use one for yourself, of course.

You'll also want to provide some padding to make writing easier and to make heavy pressure more easily visible. If you're not using a pad, use a few extra sheets of paper or some kind of synthetic writing surface (or a desk pad). If you're using paper for padding, then check the top sheet of padding after every analysis. If the writer wrote with heavy pressure, the padding may be indented, which can be a bit of an annoyance for the next writer. Put the indented sheet(s) on the bottom and when all the sheets have been used up, take them home to use as scrap paper.

The pen should be a good quality ballpoint pen, and you'll want to carry one or two spares as well as a few refills or additional pens. Choose a model that won't slip easily but isn't so deeply etched that it will be uncomfortable for some people. Or have a variety of models that the writer can choose.

Check your pens regularly to make sure that they write well and have sufficient ink. Whenever you're setting up to do readings, check that your pens write properly and wipe excess ink off the tip, if necessary.

Writers are free to use their own writing instrument or the pen that you provide—it's their choice. Be clear about this when you hand them a pen. You could say something like: "Here's a pen, if you need one", or something similar. Some day, you may well meet someone who'll turn down your pen and pull out a gold-tipped fountain pen instead.

Setting

A good handwriting sample is one that is written as freely and naturally as possible. This requires comfortable seating, a cleared table, good lighting and lots of space. Nothing should restrict the writer's motions; there should be plenty of elbow room and personal space so that the writer doesn't feel crowded. If circumstances prevent this, you'll have to improvise. At least make sure that the setting allows the writer's writing hand and arm to move freely. Remember to accommodate left-handed writers as well.

Not all venues are well lit, so it's a good idea to pack a small desk lamp, in case you have access to an electrical outlet, as well as a small, battery-powered lamp, such as a reading light. These are designed to be clipped onto a book or its cover, and can thus be used on a clipboard, but it's best to get a model that can also stand on the table on its own, so that it doesn't get in the way of the writer who likes to write with the sheet flat on the table. Check the batteries regularly and always carry a spare set or two with you.

Instructions to the writer

Have the writer sit comfortably at the table. She can write anything she wants, preferably several lines of text, and take as long as she likes. Since some people can't think of anything to write when put on the spot, offer a few sample texts printed on a sheet or two. Anything that's emotionally neutral will do: a short passage from a novel, newspaper or magazine article, a letter to a friend, and so on. The text should not contain any strongly emotional content so as not to trigger a reaction, since anger, sadness, and so on, can change a person's handwriting. The sample texts should be printed in fairly large letters for visibility.

Offer a pen, as described above, and ask the person to write in long-hand, explaining that cursive writing gives the best results. If she says that she doesn't write in cursive, tell her to write the way she normally does. If she says that she has several ways of writing, tell her to use the handwriting she uses the most—preferably cursive, of course.

When she's ready to start, give her some space and privacy: make sure she doesn't feel rushed and don't stare. As soon as she's she's finished writing, give her your full attention and proceed with the reading.

Tools

While doing the analysis, it's a good idea to use a magnifying glass, whether you need one or not. It's a tool of the trade, after all, so it will make you look more professional. If it's strictly for show, get a large, standard shaped one, with a round or rectangular lens and a full-size handle. Invest in a good one to increase the impression of professionalism. If you like to explain what you're doing, get one that's large enough for both you and the writer to look at the handwriting at the same time. It's expected that you handle it expertly; spend some time practicing with a friend so that you know how to hold it and position it so that you can both see clearly.

Whether you want to go to the trouble of using the other tools is up to you. Use them if you want to make the analysis as accurate as possible, to lengthen the time spent on a reading, or simply to appear more professional. If you use them, make sure that you're comfortable handling them, alone and in conjunction with the magnifying glass.

The actual reading

This is where you deliver the goods: you're going to go through the writer's handwriting and make her feel good about herself. You want her to remember you as a warm, likeable person, interested and compassionate. This makes the experience satisfying for her and helps pave the way for repeat engagements. You do this by making her the centre of attention; the handwriting and the analysis are secondary. There's no need to go overboard; just be friendly and non-judgemental.

Do the analysis. If you like, point out every sign that you're analysing and explain its meaning, then make a note of it on the tick sheet (described below). For example: "*Your writing slants to the right. This means that you're a sociable person. You like people; you relate to others and like to be around them.*" Face the writer and make eye contact as often as possible while doing the analysis. The idea is to make her feel that you're having a conversation with her and taking notes incidentally, not that you're taking inventory.

You can make the reading as long or as short as you like. Depending on circumstances—the kind of setting, the length of the line-up, time constraints, and so on—you can do a reading that lasts as little as two minutes or as long as five minutes, and even longer if you're a good talker.

If you don't have much time, state the point very briefly in two different ways—this helps ensure that the writer understands. For example: "*You're a sociable person; you like to be around people.*"

If you have more time, develop the idea more fully. State the point in several ways and give examples, e.g.: "*You're a sociable person. You like being around people; you enjoy the company of others. You probably have many friends and you like to spend time with them. Perhaps you like going to the movies with a group, or maybe you prefer to chat with your best friend over coffee. In any case, I have a feeling that you like to do things with other people. Chances are that you enjoy family gatherings and parties as well."*

There's no need to memorize whole paragraphs; you only have to understand the trait and use a bit of imagination. Describe the trait and find an example or two of how it might manifest itself. You can use the sample descriptions in the next section to get you started. As time goes on, you will gain experience and soon you'll develop your own style.

Take your time with the reading; don't rush through it. With experience, you'll get a sense of how long you can go on before the writer has had enough. People love to hear about themselves and will listen to every word you say, so they may be more patient than you think! Still, it's a good idea to leave them wanting more. Just a little.

When you're done, you may answer any questions the writer has, if you have the time and the setting allows it. Then hand her the tick sheet—and a business card she can give to a friend, if you like—thank her and move on to the next person.

Sample lines

Here are samples of long descriptions for every trait in the system. You can use them as given or as a starting point for your own explanations. Some readers like to memorize lines; others prefer to memorize the essence of the interpretations and ad lib.

Slant

Right: *"You're a sociable person. You like being around people; you enjoy the company of others. You probably have many friends and you like to spend time with them. You have empathy for the feelings of others. You probably enjoy family gatherings and parties as well."*

Vertical: *"You are just as happy being around people as you are being alone. You may enjoy the company of others, but you're not particularly drawn to them. You like to keep a certain distance. Your head rules over your heart: you make decisions based on your thinking, not your feelings. You probably enjoy a good book, a movie or a long walk."*

Left: *"You're a bit of a lone wolf. You would rather go for a walk—alone— than to a party. You keep your distance and don't get drawn into the emotions of others. You would probably be happy living on a desert island, alone with your thoughts or a good book."*

Variable: *"You like to be around people, but you also enjoy being alone. It changes; sometimes you want to party and sometimes you want to lock yourself in a room and watch television or read a book."*

Margins

Narrow left: *"You have a conservative outlook. In your personal life, your past is important to you. In your professional life and in your interests, you believe in the proven, the tried-and-true. You have little or no interest in the new and novel, in the 'latest and greatest', in the cutting edge."*

Centred: *"You have a good balance between the past and the future. Your past experiences are valuable to you; you draw wisdom from them. At the same time, you have an eye to the future, which looks bright to you. You have no problem moving forward and, if something new comes along, you happily accept it if you think it's worthwhile."*

Narrow right: *"You have a progressive outlook. You leave the past behind you and move forward. The future is bright. You like to be at the cutting edge of things. You're first in line to try the latest tool, technique or gadget."*

Variable: *"Sometimes you feel drawn to the past, at other times you feel drawn toward the future. One day, you may wish that things were the way they were a long time ago; the next day, you can't wait for things to change, as if tomorrow can't come fast enough for you."*

Word spacing

Wide: *"You need time and space to yourself. If you spend much time around other people, you feel crowded, maybe even like you're gasping for air. Then you need to take some time out by being alone."*

Average: *"You enjoy being around other people, but at some point, you need some time and space to yourself. You can get close to others as long as they don't crowd you too much."*

Narrow: *"You can't get enough of other people. You never tire of interacting with them, of getting close to them. Between being alone or with others, you'd much rather choose company."*

Baseline
Horizontal: *"You're not easily pulled off course. Once you start something, you see it through."*
Rising: *"You have an optimistic outlook. You're generally a happy person."*
Falling: *"You have a pretty realistic outlook on life. You're not easily disappointed."*
Concave: *"You're enthusiastic about starting new things."*
Convex: *"You may find it difficult to start new things, but once you've started, you become enthusiastic and see things through."*
Words are rising: *"You have a lot of courage. You put much effort into doing things right."*
Words are falling: *"You feel like you're constantly struggling."*
Uneven: *"Your outlook changes. You are optimistic at times, pessimistic at other times."*
Wavy: *"You adapt easily to whatever situation presents itself to you."*

Size
Large: *"You always get noticed. You stand out in a crowd. You're the centre of attention, the life of the party. You draw people to you, either because of what you do or who you are—or perhaps a combination of both."*
Average: *"You enjoy being an active participant in a group of equals. You're a team player. You like the exchange of information and you like working together. You want your voice to be heard but you don't feel the need to be heard all the time."*
Small: *"There's more to you than most people realize. You don't like to be noticed; in fact, you may prefer to be invisible. When you join a group, you're quite happy to just watch, listen and absorb; you don't talk about yourself or your opinions. You have no desire to be famous. You prefer to work behind the scenes and let others get the glory."*

Capitals
Large: *"You have a strong sense of self, of your identity. You're proud of who you are and of what you've done, and you command the respect you deserve from others. If people you meet don't know you or your accomplishments, you tell them."*

Average: *"You know who you are and you accept yourself. You don't feel that you're better or worse than anybody else. You know your strengths and weaknesses and act accordingly. You're confident and in control when you meet new people. You don't need to prove yourself to others."*

Small: *"You're modest and unassuming. There's more to you than meets the eye; you don't feel that it's necessary for others to know of your accomplishments. When you join a group, you may remain silent for a long time and people may not notice you. If you're well known in some circle, it's very likely that even your friends don't know about it."*

Pressure

Heavy: *"You have a lot of drive. You have the energy to accomplish just about anything you want and you're probably very successful in your undertakings."*

Medium: *"You have a healthy amount of drive. You have the energy to accomplish your goals and enough left over to enjoy other activities. You're probably quite successful in your undertakings."*

Light: *"You're a very accepting person. You prefer to go with the flow, rather than trying to change things."*

Connectedness

Connected: *"You have a very logical mind. You think things through. When you're dealing with a problem, you look at every piece in turn, assembling them, like a puzzle, until you see the whole picture and find the solution. If it's necessary, you're able to retrace every step you took in your thinking."*

Grouped: *"You are both logical and intuitive. You think, but you also grasp without thinking—at least, not consciously. When you're trying to solve a problem, you examine a few pieces and put them together in logical order. But you also stop thinking at times, and when you do, big chunks of the solution pop into your mind, apparently out of nowhere."*

Disconnected: *"You are very intuitive. When you focus on a problem, you look at all the pieces in no particular order. You jump around a lot: you examine this piece, then that one, then maybe back to the first one, and so on. After a while, without any effort on your part, the complete solution suddenly appears to you."*

Connections

Garland: *"You're a warm and friendly person. You're open with your feelings and you respond to the feelings of others. If someone needs a hug or a shoulder to cry on, you're the one they go to."*

Arcade: *"You are rather reserved. Although you're sensitive, you don't like to show your feelings; you keep them to yourself. You prefer to keep others at a safe distance."*

Angular: *"You deal with people according to your beliefs and principles. You expect people to live up to expectations, and if they don't, they have only themselves to blame."*

Thready: *"You're a very diplomatic person. You make people feel good; sometimes you may even tell them what they want to hear."*

Simplicity

Simplified: *"You're a clear thinker. When you look at a problem or situation, you grasp it immediately and see what's important and what isn't. You see the big picture. You deal with the situation effectively and efficiently, with minimum effort."*

Simple: *"You're a practical thinker. When you look at a situation or a problem, you grasp the big picture without losing track of the important details. You find practical solutions—solutions that work for everyone or everything involved."*

Complicated: *"You are very detail-minded. You pay close attention to the little details because you understand how important they are. You leave no stone unturned. You're not happy until even the smallest thing is taken care of."*

Originality

Original: *"You're a distinct individual. You stand out simply by being yourself. You have your own beliefs; you don't necessarily think what everybody else is thinking or act the way everybody else acts. You live your life in your own way, creatively."*

Conforming: *"You like to be part of a group. You would rather fit in than stand out in any way. You know that the majority is right and you draw strength from that knowledge. You like to keep up on the latest trends."*

Dominant zone

Upper: *"You are motivated primarily by your mind. You're a thinker; you have imagination and vision. You have high ideals and ambitions. You dream of a better future, a better world, a better you, and you want to realize those dreams."*

Middle: *"You are motivated primarily by your feelings. Everything you see, everything that happens around you, leaves an impression on you, and you react to it. You enjoy the moment and you focus on daily living: work, responsibilities, home, family, friends, etc., are important to you."*

Lower: *"You are motivated primarily by your body and by the world around you. You like feeling your body: you enjoy physical activity, food, or working with your hands. You are interested in the physical world: perhaps you like to build things, or you enjoy making money. You may be involved in business, real estate or construction, or perhaps in mechanical things."*

THE STROLLING READING

There is very little difference between doing readings and performing close-up magic or mentalism in walkaround and table-hopping situations. You approach an individual or a group, introduce yourself, perform, exit gracefully and move on to the next person or group. Like all close-up performances, it's as much about the interaction as it is about your specialty. If you're a sociable person yourself, chances are that strolling readings will become your favourite kind of work. You get paid, in essence, to spend an evening meeting people, interacting with them, and handing out your business card.

The writer writes a single long word (e.g., "Immediately"), a short sentence (e.g., "My name is" and her name), or her signature on a card, business card to postcard size. The tick sheet and contact information are printed below the writing space or on the back of the card.

If the writer is standing and the cards are fairly small, you hand her a thick stack of cards so that she has a reasonably rigid writing surface. If she's sitting at a table, you hand her a thin stack, enough to provide padding without being uncomfortably thick. Business card holders, although they add a touch of class, are more of a hindrance than a help. For larger cards, you use a small clipboard. It keeps the cards flat and gives the writer extra space and flexibility.

When she's finished writing, you get the pen and cards back and go straight into the reading. You use the magnifying glass if you like; it wouldn't make sense to use any of the other tools here.

Typically, you analyse three to six signs. The lines you deliver for each sign can be as long or as short as you like, and as time and the writer's interest dictate. You mark the results on the tick sheet as you go along; when you've finished, you answer any questions she may have, deliver a sales message if you feel it's appropriate, hand her the card and move on to the next spectator.

TICK SHEETS

There are several ways to record the findings of a graphological analysis, ranging from a written report to sophisticated charts such as 'psychograms' and 'radar graphs'. For our purposes, the simplest and most convenient tool is a tick sheet, a list of all the signs analysed and the possible interpretations for each one. You simply circle, underline or check off the ones that apply.

Tick sheet formats

The standard tick sheet lists all the signs, each one broken down into a list of interpretations, one per line:

Slant: Sociability
☐ *Sociable, responsive, interested in others*
☐ *Practical, independent, head rules over heart*
☐ *Cautious, reserved, observant*
☐ *Ambivalent, moods vary*

If more space is available, the interpretations can be expanded into short explanatory paragraphs:

Slant: Sociability
☐ *Sociable*
   You are a sociable person. You like others and you respond to
   their emotions.
☐ *Neutral*
   You are a practical person. You are independent; your head
   rules over your heart. You like people but aren't drawn into
   their emotional states.
☐ *Solitary*
   You're cautious around others. You tend to be reserved and
   you prefer to observe than to interact.
☐ *Varying*
   You're ambivalent about others. You like to be around people
   at times, but you like to be left alone at other times.

Conversely, if space is lacking, interpretations can be condensed to
one or two words and strung together onto a single line per sign, separated by a 'middle dot', a dash or a slash:

Sociability
Sociable • Neutral • Solitary • Varying

The standard tick sheet can be vastly improved upon simply by grouping related traits together into meaningful categories. This turns it into
a rudimentary psychological profile, which is far more interesting and
useful to the writer than a mere collection of traits in random order, yet
requires no extra work.

WHO YOU ARE
Motivation (Zone)
   Mind, ideals • Emotions, daily life • Instincts, physical world
Drive (Pressure)
   Driven • Healthy • Accepting
Individuality (Originality)
   Individual • Group

YOU AND OTHERS
Sociability (Slant)
  Sociable • Neutral • Solitary • Varying
Presence (Size)
  Stands out • Blends in • Reserved
Recognition (Capitals)
  Likes recognition • Confident • Modest
Interaction (Connections)
  Responsive • Reserved • Principled • Diplomatic
Need for space (Word spacing)
  Low • Normal • High

YOU AND THE WORLD
Internal processing (Connectedness)
  Logical • Mixed • Intuitive
Problem solving (Simplicity)
  Big picture • Practical • Detail-minded
Mood (Baseline)
  Calm • Optimistic • Pessimistic • Varying
  Quick enthusiasm • Progressive enthusiasm
  Courageous • Burdened
Past and future (Margins)
  Conservative • Mixed • Progressive • Variable

Full-size tick sheets

For formal readings, a trifold brochure is an ideal handout. This is a letter-size sheet, blank on one side, that folds into an elegant, professional-looking brochure. It has a cover with your marketing message, a tick sheet, and the handwriting sample.

Trifold brochures are very easy to make with a computer and printer. Later on, you can have one professionally designed and printed. Open your word processor and create a new document, letter size, landscape mode, margins of ½ inch all around. Divide the page into three columns with a ½ inch gutter between the columns (in the illustration, the columns are outlined for clarity only). Adjust the width of the columns as follows: the leftmost column is 2¾ inches wide, the middle one is 3¼ inches wide, the rightmost is 3 inches wide. The inner flap—the leftmost panel—is slightly narrower than the two other panels to allow for a margin of error when making the fold.

3"

What does your *Handwriting* reveal?

Your handwriting is as unique as you are. Graphology, or Handwriting Analysis, helps you to get to know yourself.

For your next party or corporate event, give your guests a unique experience! Call

John Quill Graphologist
(212) 345-6789 • http://johnquill.com

←fold

3¼"

YOU AND THE WORLD

Internal processing (connectedness)
☐☐☐ Logical
☐☐☐ Mixed
☐☐☐ Intuitive

Problem solving (simplicity)
☐☐☐ Big picture
☐☐☐ Practical
☐☐☐ Detail-minded

Mood (baseline)
☐☐☐ Calm
☐☐☐ Optimistic
☐☐☐ Pessimistic
☐☐☐ Varying
☐☐☐ Quick enthusiasm
☐☐☐ Progressive enthusiasm
☐☐☐ Courageous
☐☐☐ Burdened

Past and future (margins)
☐☐☐ Conservative
☐☐☐ Mixed
☐☐☐ Progressive
☐☐☐ Variable

COMMENTS

½" margin all around

fold→

2¾"

WHO YOU ARE

Motivation (zone)
☐☐☐ Mind, ideals
☐☐☐ Emotions, daily life
☐☐☐ Instinct, physical world

Drive (pressure)
☐☐☐ Driven
☐☐☐ Healthy
☐☐☐ Accepting

Individuality (originality)
☐☐☐ Individual
☐☐☐ Group

YOU AND OTHERS

Sociability (slant)
☐☐☐ Sociable
☐☐☐ Neutral
☐☐☐ Solitary
☐☐☐ Varying

Presence (size)
☐☐☐ Stands out
☐☐☐ Blends in
☐☐☐ Reserved

Recognition (capitals)
☐☐☐ Likes recognition
☐☐☐ Confident
☐☐☐ Modest

Interaction (connections)
☐☐☐ Responsive
☐☐☐ Reserved
☐☐☐ Principled
☐☐☐ Diplomatic

Need for space (word spacing)
☐☐☐ Low
☐☐☐ Normal
☐☐☐ High

Enter the tick sheet information starting in the left column and continuing in the middle column. Below the end of the tick sheet, add a few lines for comments. If you have some space left, you can put your contact information (or space for your agent's) below the comments, otherwise they go at the bottom of the right panel, which is the cover. It contains your headline and marketing message. For a nice touch, add a box in which to write the writer's name and the date of the analysis.

Print a copy and see how it looks. If one edge of the writing is cut off, shift the content of the page by increasing the margin at that end and decreasing it by the same amount at the other. If both ends are cut off, increase both margins and decrease the width of the gutters by the same amount. Repeat until the sheet prints properly. Fold the sheet as described below and adjust the content of the rightmost column—the cover—so that it looks centred, if necessary.

Print out a small number of sheets. It's a good idea to mark them so that you know where to make the first fold. The second fold goes to the edge of the first fold, so it doesn't have to be marked. Stack the sheets and put the pile in front of you so that the blank side is up and the tick sheet end is nearest you. Square the pile carefully. With a ruler, measure 4 inches from the top of the sheet, and draw a pencil line across the edges of all the sheets, on one side. The brochures are ready to be used. Store them flat in your case, in a clipboard or folder.

When doing readings, the writer writes on the blank side of the sheet, with the cover end at the top. After she's finished writing, you do the analysis and fill out the tick sheet, then you fold the sheet as follows. Place it on the table in front of you so that the text is facing you and right side up. Bring the bottom edge up to the pencil mark or slightly above it, make sure the fold is straight and make the crease. Rotate the sheet 180° horizontally, bring the edge nearest you up to the fold and make the crease. Your trifold is ready to be handed to the writer.

Other designs are possible. For example, a single-fold brochure, made of a legal-size sheet cut in half (you make two brochures from a single sheet). Each half sheet is then folded in half. You have a cover panel on the front, a marketing and contact information panel on the back, and the tick sheet, with space for comments, on the two inner panels. This style of brochure can be pre-folded, since the writer writes on a separate sheet of paper.

It's up to you whether to include the names of the signs (e.g., 'Zone', 'Pressure', 'Originality', and so on) on the tick sheet or leave them out. You can certainly put them in when you're starting to do readings, as a reminder, and remove them later on, when you have experience and no longer need them to jog your memory.

Comments

The Comments section is one of your most powerful secret weapons for building rapport. People love to be flattered; anything you say that makes them feel special is guaranteed to make them remember you in a positive way. In the words of the poet Maya Angelou: *"People will forget what you said, people will forget what you did, but people will never forget how you made them feel."*

Find a trait or two that stands out and write something positive about it. For example, for a right slant or garland connections, you can write *"Very friendly; a people person"*; for vertical writing, *"Reason prevails!"*; for a left slant, perhaps something like *"You like to walk alone"*. You can write *"I envy you your optimism!"* (or cheerfulness, if that's how the writer comes across) for a sharply rising baseline. *"You're the life of the party"* for large writing, *"You're a go-getter"* for heavy pressure, *"Highly logical mind"* for very connected writing, and so on. You should be able to find something flattering to write for most traits; you can use the sample lines given elsewhere for inspiration. If all else fails, if you really can't find anything interesting in a handwriting, you can always write: *"It was an honour to 'read' you!"* or something similar. It sounds flattering, it's warm and it's friendly.

Mini-tick sheets and teasers

The condensed style of tick sheet is compact enough that you can list several signs on a business card and still have space left for your contact information and a sample of handwriting. You can have everything printed on one side only, or print the tick sheet on one side and contact information on the other, close to the edge so as to leave as much space as possible for the writing sample. The two-sided card gives you space for more signs on the tick sheet.

What your handwriting says about you
Are you sociable? Sociable / Neutral / Distant / Variable
You are motivated by your: Mind / Emotions / Instincts
In a crowd, you: Stand out / Blend in / Observe
You like to be: Noticed / Yourself / Unnoticed

Intrigued? Try something different for your next event!

John Quill, Graphologist
(212) 345-6789 • http://johnquill.com

What does your handwriting say about you?

Intrigued? Try something different for your next event!
John Quill, Graphologist • (212) 345-6789 • johnquill.com

A folded business card design gives you additional space for your marketing message. It's a card twice the height of a standard business card that you fold in half before you hand it out. On the outside, it looks like a business card with an expanded marketing message on the back. On the inside, the top half is left blank for the writing sample, the bottom half contains the tick sheet.

The same design can be used for larger cards, index card or postcard size (a quarter of standard letter size). These give the writer more space to write and allow for a standard-format tick sheet, rather than a condensed one. When folded, they're still small enough to be slipped comfortably into a purse or pocket.

How sociable are you?
☐ *Sociable, interested*
☐ *Neutral, independent*
☐ *Cautious, reserved*
☐ *Ambivalent, variable*

How do you deal with others?
☐ *Responsive*
☐ *Reserved, detached*
☐ *Principled*
☐ *Diplomatic*

In a crowd, you:
☐ *Stand out*
☐ *Blend in*
☐ *Are reserved*

Are you logical or intuitive?
☐ *Logical*
☐ *Mixed*
☐ *Intuitive*

You prefer to be:
☐ *The center of attention*
☐ *Confident, yourself*
☐ *Unnoticed*

What motivates you?
☐ *Mind, ideals*
☐ *Emotions, daily living*
☐ *Instinct, body, physical world*

The choice of signs to include in a mini-ticksheet is up to you. With the exception of margins, word spacing, and baseline—which are likely to be meaningless in a small writing area—any combination of signs can be used. For analysing text, one approach is to look only at signs that have to do with interpersonal relationships (slant, size, capitals, connections). Another approach is to take one or two signs from each of the categories described above (self, others, world). For analysing signatures, you can look at ambition (the baseline is much more reliable in a signature), and self versus upbringing (capitals), plus whichever other signs you choose. It's a good idea to limit the number of signs analyzed to perhaps four, so that the writer feels that she's getting her money's worth should she hire you for a full reading.

Because of the informality of strolling readings, you can be a bit more playful in the wording of the tick sheet. For example, instead of: "Are you original or conforming?", you can write: "Do you follow trends or do you set them?" It also has less of a sting, an important consideration when the reading is delivered in front of a group, which is usually the case when strolling.

Mini-ticksheets are also useful for impromptu readings that you can do any time, anywhere, as long as you have your business cards with you. Such readings are an excellent way to break the ice when meeting people and to drum up business. In just about any situation, if you can find a way to turn the conversation toward psychology, human behaviour, handwriting, graphology—or to parties and other social events—you can do a quick analysis and get a foot in the door. It's a great giveaway that people will keep, as well as an incentive for them to hire you.

Impromptu readings intended to gain publicity or to drum up business can be done on as little as a single sign. You use a 'teaser' card, designed specifically for this purpose. It's a business card, single- or double-sided, with a bold heading that doubles as the ticksheet, space for a handwriting sample, and contact and marketing information.

Are you an

EXTROVERT or an INTROVERT
(people-person)　　　　　　　　　　(loner)

?

Intrigued? Try something different for your next event!
John Quill, Graphologist
(212) 345-6789 • http://johnquill.com

Are you a PEOPLE-PERSON or a LONER?
Write a word or two in the space below and I will tell you!

Intrigued? Try something different for your next event!
John Quill, Graphologist
(212) 345-6789 • http://johnquill.com

The slant is an excellent sign to use on a teaser, with a caption like: "Are you a people-person or a loner?" Anything written will be enough to determine the slant, and voilà—almost instant reading! If circumstances warrant it, you can do a whole room in just a few minutes. Hand out the cards, have everybody write something—anything at all—then go around, glance at the slant and circle the appropriate interpretation (for vertical writing, draw a line between the two and tell the writer that she's in between; for variable writing, circle both and explain that her sociability varies). This is very powerful: you do something with every person in the room or at a table, and leave them with something they'll want to keep—which also happens to contain your contact information for future business.

Markets

MARKETS

Since you're a magician or a mentalist, you already know a lot about different kinds of performances and the venues at which you can present them. Here are a few common and not so common venues and ways in which you can use graphology.

VENUES AND OPPORTUNITIES

Fairs

Of the many kinds of venues at which you can do readings, among the simplest and easiest to do are fairs and exhibitions. Look around and you'll find flea markets and street fairs, malls and trade exhibits, psychic and agricultural fairs, and all manner of special events at which you can rent a booth, hang up a sign and sell your services. You only need some signage and two chairs—and make sure that you bring plenty of tick-sheets, extra clipboards and pens.

Aside from doing the readings, you'll probably have to spend some time standing in front of the table and talking to passers-by to drum up business, or have someone else do it for you. But with any luck—and weather permitting, if it's an outdoor fair—you can make a few hundred dollars easily at these kinds of events.

Since your deliverables—the tick sheet—contains your marketing and contact information, and since people are very unlikely to throw out something as personal and personalized as an analysis of their own handwriting, everybody who gets a reading leaves with your information in hand. You never know when someone will have a family event—or even a corporate one—at which a graphologist would be welcome. After doing a reading, you can pitch mail-in readings (see below) for the writer's friends, relatives, colleagues, and so on, and 'pitch books', inexpensive booklets on some very basic aspect of graphology.

If you're very busy and have some extra table space, get a few more chairs so that you can have several people writing at the same time, instead of waiting in line. People are less likely to get impatient and leave, and you can do more readings in the same amount of time.

Many fairs also feature live entertainment. You may be able to sell your stage show at the same event. If it features a graphology presentation, you can entice people to visit your booth afterward for a full reading.

Corporate and private events

Corporate events, such as receptions, parties, casino nights, company picnics and the like, are even easier to do. They give you the same advantages as fairs with less work. You get paid a flat fee, whether you do one reading or a hundred, and you don't have to convince guests to part with their money, since what you offer is free.

The nature of the event and the venue will determine whether you do strolling or full readings. The latter are handled exactly as for fairs.

Corporate events often feature stage performances as well. You can sell your magic or mentalism act as part of the package and use it to help generate interest in readings after the show.

Personal celebrations, such as weddings, anniversaries, bar mitzvahs and the like, are very similar in all respects. The only difference is that you're not likely to be asked to do full readings.

Trade shows

Trade shows are among the most demanding venues but also the most lucrative. You get hired by the day and work all day long, often on your feet, for which you get paid handsomely. It's not so easy to get into this field, but once you're in and you've proven your worth to the exhibitors, you're likely to get repeat engagements and you'll have a foot in the door for working other trade shows.

Trade shows are like fairs in which companies exhibit their wares to professionals in a specific field. For example, at a printing equipment trade show, companies that manufacture printing presses, scanners, inks, paper, and so on, show off their products and services to people who work in the printing industry.

Exhibitors want to deliver sales pitches and discuss the prospects' needs in order to sell to them. But first, they have to attract them to their booth, and that's not so easy. If there are a dozen ink manufacturers, for example, why go to one rather than another?

One solution is to hire an entertainer to attract attention and generate interest. Many companies hire magicians and mentalists—as well as jugglers, acrobats and all kinds of performance artists—to draw a crowd. A novel approach is to hire a graphologist to give brief signature analyses.

The graphologist has an advantage here that other entertainers do not: he's already interacting with the prospect. Now it's only a tiny step to get the prospect's contact information, which the exhibitor will then use to follow up for a potential sale. This is your strong point for getting hired. The more people want their signature analysed, the more names of prospects or potential prospects the exhibitor gets.

While you're negotiating to provide your graphology services to the exhibitor, you can also try to sell your magic or mentalism show as a further attention-getter.

Hospitality suites

A hospitality suite is a bit like a private lounge in which staff and selected guests can meet and shmooze in the evening, after the convention or trade show closes. Typically, you'll find snacks and drinks—and sometimes entertainment too.

Both magic and mentalism work well in hospitality suites, as do readings. The sponsor decides what you should do. If you're going to include readings, whether incidental readings during a performance or full readings, it's a good idea to make it known that you will be handing out business cards, just in case the sponsor objects to this.

Unlike most other venues, you do not try to attract spectators in a hospitality suite setting. You're simply one of the fixtures, so to speak, rather like the barman behind the bar. Don't ask people whether they want to see something or other; let them come to you and ask. They'll spread the word and soon, others will come to your table to see you work.

Although you'll be working at a table, hospitality suite work is somewhat like strolling entertainment at cocktail parties in the sense that people can come and go at any time, even in the middle of a trick. It's wise therefore to keep sets short, between five and ten minutes, to choose tricks that stand on their own, rather than tricks that follow from the outcome of a previous trick, and to have quite a variety of material, so that spectators who come by your table more than once are less likely to see the same tricks performed every time.

Magic and mentalism performances

Whenever you perform close-up magic or any kind of mentalism, you have an opportunity to introduce graphology into your act. This can be anything from a single incidental reading in the course of a trick or mental experiment, to a closing effect centred around graphology.

At the very least, you'll likely get a few requests for readings at the end of your act. If you go all out by closing with an effect that leaves your business card in every spectator's hand, you may get booked in the future or even hired on the spot.

The teaser card described above is perfect for this. You do a reading on a single sign for every spectator at the table or in the group and leave them with your card. If you want to do something more mysterious, you can turn it into a simple version of 'Pseudo-Psychometry'. You turn away while everybody writes, then a spectator collects all the cards, mixes them and hands you the stack. You do the reading for each card and end by handing the cards to their respective owners. It appears that you can identify the writer from the handwriting, which is quite a powerful effect[7].

Since the presentation is about psychology, rather than psychic ability, this effect is appropriate for a magic performance. But if you like, you can extend it even further by first doing a magic trick with the cards, such as a short 'Oil and Water' or 'Follow the Leader' sequence (written versus blank cards), 'Haunted Deck' (with a stack of business cards), 'Cards through Newspaper' (also called 'Queen's Soirée', among other names), and many others. For these, you may prefer to use your standard business cards, rather than teaser cards, so that the readings come as a complete surprise; just be sure that graphology is listed on the card as one of your skills.

Close-up magic or mentalism with the addition of graphology is an excellent combination: it has all the advantages of a close-up performance, plus the extra draw of personalized readings. People get enter-

---

7   See 'Pentachrome' in the Mentalism section.

tained and an ego boost—and your card in their hands. A perfect combination for both you and the audience!

Cruise ships

If you perform magic or mentalism on cruise ships, the ability to do readings—and perhaps even lectures or classes (see below)—makes you more valuable and versatile as an entertainer.

Graphology parties

If you enjoy socializing and parties—and being surrounded by women—you'll enjoy graphology parties. They're not huge money-makers, but they'll net you some cash and a fun evening for two to three hours of work.

You go to a private residence and mingle for a while. When the hostess is ready, you give a short talk on graphology, which you can supplement with appropriate mentalism routines (dressed up as graphology, of course!). Then you hand out blank sheets (or your trifold brochure, if you use the kind that's blank inside) and explain how to write a text for analysis. When that's done, you head to a separate room where you do a full reading, in private, for each guest. Afterward, you can mingle some more and leave whenever you feel like it.

The talk at the beginning is optional, but always welcome. It sets the tone for what you're going to do, generates interest and builds excitement. You can talk for as little as five minutes or do a full half-hour show, or anything in between. Usually, the talk is part of the deal—no charge—but make sure that the hostess makes time (and space) available for it. Discuss your requirements when she books you.

At the end of the talk or while the guests are writing, you can choose the order in which you want them to come see you for their reading. Should your reading disappoint one of the first guests you see, chances are that her disappointment will spread to the others when she returns to the party and you'll have made a bad impression. To prevent this from happening, choose the most enthusiastic guests to see you first. If one of the later guests is disappointed, it won't matter anymore, because the first ones will already have spread their enthusiasm and the letdown will fall on deaf ears.

You can charge a flat fee for a party, based on your time, but it's much more common to charge per guest, at your normal price for a reading. For example, if there are six guests and you charge $30 per reading, then you make $180. Sometimes the hostess pays your fee, but usually, each guest pays for herself. Guests can pay you directly, when you do the reading, or the hostess can collect from them and pay you the whole amount, either in advance or at the end of the evening.

To make it worth your while, you'll want to set a minimum fee for parties. Let's say that you decide on $300. At $30 per reading, you'll need ten people to earn that amount. Ten will therefore be the minimum number of guests you request when you get booked for a party. Don't include the hostess, because it's common to give her a free (or heavily discounted) reading in exchange for hosting the event.

You can increase your minimum to make up for people who may have to cancel at the last minute—for example, ask for twelve guests so that you'll get at least ten—and also if circumstances justify a higher fee, such as compensation for travelling to another city.

You'll also want to set a limit on the maximum number of readings you'll do, so that everybody gets a turn and you can end at a reasonable hour. The typical range for parties is ten to twenty-five guests. Decide on how much time you want to spend doing readings and divide that by the time an average reading takes you. This will determine your upper limit. For example, in two hours of seven-minute readings, you can accommodate about seventeen guests. You'll also want to take breaks, perhaps ten minutes every hour. Make sure that the hostess knows this when she books you.

Ty Kralin, who uses graphological presentations extensively, devised a novel (and very clever) marketing tool that will help spread the word about your expertise and get you more business[8]. Have the hostess tell every guest to bring a sample signature from someone who won't attend the party. At the end of your talk, give every guest one of your business cards and a pen or pencil. For each guest in turn, do a short analysis of the signature and have the guest take notes, including the reason for each point you make. End by telling the guests to give the card to the author of the signature.

---

8   In his article in *Syzygy*, Quarterly Supplement #10.

Not only will the guests talk about this all evening, but when they hand the card to the signature's owner, it will create a minor sensation—especially if the guest embellishes the reading, which often happens—and you may well be contacted for a private consultation or a party.

Graphology parties aren't limited to private engagements. They're a natural for women's groups, social clubs, civic organizations and so on. Usually, the organization pays your fees. You can charge the same way as for private parties or a flat fee related to the expected number of guests, or you can simply treat it like any corporate event and charge according to time.

Mail-in readings

After you do a full reading, people will often tell you that they wish you could do one for so-and-so (a friend, relative, colleague, etc.), who would love to have his or her handwriting analysed but isn't present at the event. Or they may simply mention that they know some people who'd be interested in a reading. This is your cue to sell your services for parties and other events—and for mail-in readings.

Prepare a flyer—a quarter-page will do—with a short graphology marketing message and instructions for mail-in analyses. Explain that the text should be written in cursive, if at all possible, on blank, un-lined paper, that the content should be non-emotional, like a letter to a friend, and signed if you like. List the price and instructions for payment (cheque, money order, credit cards, PayPal or other online payment systems, and so on—whatever you accept) and your mailing address, and be sure to instruct the sender to provide a return address! You can even make the flyer into a form that is to be sent to you, together with the writing sample and payment. Give the writer as many sheets as she has friends who might be interested in a reading—or even a few more.

When you receive the request in the mail, do the analysis on your standard trifold tick sheet and mail it back to the sender. It contains your marketing message, so you don't need to include anything else, although you can include another mail-in flyer or two.

Charge the same amount you do for a standard reading, plus postage if you like, or ask for a self-addressed, stamped envelope. It's up to you whether you keep the writing sample or return it to the sender. If you decide to keep the samples, mention this on the flyer. If you don't and you come across an interesting sample that you want to keep for your files or for a course that you give, you can always make a photocopy.

Talks

Talks on graphology, whether you give them for free or for pay, are among your most versatile and useful tools. Free talks, given at libraries, book stores, adult education centres and so on, can generate a lot of business for you. It's advertising for your services and doesn't cost you anything but your time.

As with all advertising, start with the "what's in it for me" idea in mind. Then you'll be able to come up with talks that generate interest because they promise a benefit for the listener. People love to find out about themselves, so talk about 'What your handwriting reveals about you'. They're interested in others too, so talk about 'Reading people through their handwriting'. They like to meet others, so tell them 'How to break the ice with handwriting analysis'. And so on. Give people a reason to listen to your talk and you can generate a lot of interest.

You can re-use, adapt and expand some talks to target specific groups. For example, singles: they want to meet people, be interesting, get to know others, determine whether they're suitable partners, and so on. Singles groups are perfect, then, for your 'Reading people' and 'How to break the ice' talks. You can continue with more specialized talks, such as 'Find the man of your dreams through handwriting analysis' and 'Are you compatible?' There are several books out on graphology and relationships. They're well worth reading.

Being a showman—or show woman—you will, of course, make these talks far more interesting and entertaining than other speakers would! Think of them as lecture-demonstrations in which your magic or mentalism plays an important role. You can use tricks to illustrate the points you make, and mentalism presentations to demonstrate them. For example, a colour-changing handkerchief can be used to explain that people often expect their partner to change, but that it doesn't work (change the handkerchief back to its original colour). A version of 'Pseudo Psychometry' can be used to demonstrate how you can match a handwriting to a person. And so on.

Exactly where you draw the line between talk and show is entirely up to you. At one extreme, you can give a pure talk (with or without tricks) during which you actually impart some information about graphology. At the other extreme, you can do a full mentalism show that purports to demonstrate the power of graphology (and other aspects of human behaviour, psychology, non-verbal communication, and so on) without actually teaching the audience anything. The best solution is usually something in between: a show that also offers some genuine information. Whichever way you decide to go, just make sure that you deliver what you promise.

You can do these talks for free and offer your services for pay, on an individual basis, or you can get hired to do the whole thing—talk and readings—for a flat fee. In either case, you can sell pitch books—particularly if you have one on the specific topic you presented—and mail-in readings for a tidy profit. In addition, there's a chance that someone in the audience will want to book you for private or corporate work.

You can also do these talks at bookstores and wherever there are adult education classes. They can be used to sell books on graphology as well as classes that you give.

Classes

Aside from loving to hear about themselves, people are also very interested in learning new things. There are plenty of adult education courses, ranging from hobby interests to professional advancement courses, to prove it. An Introduction to handwriting analysis is a natural for adult education programs. Courses range from a single day or evening, to several weekends or evenings, to a whole season, usually one evening per week. Courses are usually offered in autumn, winter and spring, rarely in summer.

The simplest way to teach a course is to follow a good book. Find an introductory text on graphology—raid your local library first, so that you can work through several books until you find one that you like— and draw up a lesson plan that follows the book closely. Just make sure that the book is still in print. The lesson plan will be the outline of your course, and the book—which you can buy wholesale and sell to students for a small profit—will be the course's textbook.

If the course lasts longer than a single session, it's a good idea to give the students exercises for the following class. If the book you're following doesn't have exercises, make some up. You'll need to collect handwriting samples for this.

Feel free to perform the occasional trick in class, but remember that you're teaching graphology, so it's best to avoid tricks that are too impossible or incredible for what you're teaching.

Just as for the talks, you can slant courses in any direction you like, such as 'Breaking the ice' or 'Finding a perfect mate'. If you can come up with courses that are dissimilar enough, you may even be able to offer more than one course at a time, or over time.

PROFESSIONAL CONSIDERATIONS

Exiting gracefully

When working at fairs or other venues in which people line up for a reading, you will find it very difficult to take a break or to close for the day, because people will be lining up for your services constantly. You need a way to turn people away and either let them know when you'll be back, if taking a break, or that you're closing.

An assistant or a staff member willing to help can stand at the end of the line and turn away newcomers. Failing that, you could ask the last person in line to do the same. Alternatively, if you have a stand of some kind, you can put up a sign behind the last person in line.

Challenges

Although it's rare, you may get challenged by a spectator, writer, or even a passer-by, for instance at a fair. It could be about graphology as a whole, or it could be about something you said in a reading. Here are some bits that you may be able to use.

Graphology is based on character analysis. Although this was scientifically studied at one time, modern psychology has moved away from character analysis entirely. This is one of the main reasons that graphology has fallen out of favour among psychologists. That choice doesn't invalidate graphology, nor the field of character analysis.

The kind of analysis described here, even in the case of formal readings, is fairly basic. People are very complex; to create a more detailed and accurate psychological outline requires a professional analysis, which is much more time-consuming and costly.

A person's handwriting changes over time. Not only in the long run, but also from moment to moment. For example, a pessimistic person may write with a rising baseline when going to a fair or a party because it's a pleasurable experience; a person with a dominant lower zone may have an enlarged upper zone after listening to a talk about the environment; and so on. Therefore, anything you say about the writer only applies to the time at which the piece you analysed was written.

For entertainment purposes, all the traits are described in a neutral or positive way. Should a person insist on knowing the real meaning of a sign, you can briefly explain that you only give positive readings, since this is for entertainment only.

The system described in this book is based on a combination of the French, German and American schools of graphology. Some signs are interpreted slightly differently by the different systems; in fact, even graphologists who have studied the same system don't always agree on the meaning of certain signs. Should you happen to come across a person who knows a little bit about graphology and challenges an interpretation, you can point this out.

Giving advice

Once in a while, after doing a full reading, a writer may ask for your advice in some personal matter. In such a case, it's best to refer the writer to a professional; you don't want to be responsible for another person's life and even risk a lawsuit. Professional graphologists and other counsellors have diplomas, insurance, professional associations to back them up, and so forth, in case they give bad advice. Entertainers do not.

You could associate with a professional graphologist—and other professionals—in your area for this reason and also to generate an occasional fee for virtually no work. Should you be asked to do a comprehensive analysis or to give professional advice, you can say that you're too busy doing talks and shows and refer the person to the professional. In turn, the professional pays you a commission for getting a new customer—a referral fee. It's a win-win situation for both parties.

Getting organized

If you're a magician, chances are that you'll keep your magic and graphology work fairly separate because the two fields aren't strongly related. The market for magic performances is quite different from the market for readings, so you'll most likely have different promotional materials for the two, you'll advertise them differently, you'll have separate mailing lists, and so on. Of course, you can always promote one while doing the other. Brief readings during performances will get people to ask you for a reading afterward, at which point you can not only do a few readings, if you so choose, but also talk about your graphology services and maybe even get hired then and there. And when doing readings, you can certainly do an appropriate magic trick or two to make it known that you do magic as well, if you so desire.

If you're a mentalist, you can readily integrate graphology into your work, especially if you present yourself as an expert in human behaviour, rather than a psychic. Then the two fields essentially merge, one being an extension of the other. This allows you to promote them together, to the same market, for essentially the same clients.

Mentalism

MENTALISM

The most basic way to introduce the idea of handwriting analysis into an act is with incidental readings. There are many opportunities to do this, because so many mentalism experiments require spectators to write something. You only have to deliver one or two readings to prove that you can determine character traits just by looking at people's handwriting.

But there are things you can do to show that your skill extends well beyond mere character analysis. If, for example, you can prove that you can determine whether a written statement is true or false just by looking at it, then clearly you must be in the same league as the handwriting experts on police shows. This increases your prestige instantly and makes you more believable.

You can go even further than that. If you create the illusion that you understand many aspects of human behaviour and are able to combine them synergistically, it's very likely that you'll achieve a sort of 'Houdini effect'. Just like his numerous escapes earned him the reputation of being able to escape from any restraint, you can be seen as someone for whom human behaviour has no secrets. An enviable reputation!

How far you want to take this is entirely up to you. The presentations described in this chapter remain reasonably faithful to actual graphology, stretching it only enough to imply that it can bridge the gap to other aspects of psychology. If you're so inclined, you can stretch the truth as much as you like, for example by augmenting your readings with whatever you can glean from cold reading or even pre-show work, and crediting graphology for revealing this information. However, if you do full graphology readings as well, it would be wise to make more conservative claims about handwriting analysis, otherwise you risk being asked questions that could only be answered by a psychic!

Below are a few examples of mentalism experiments adapted to graphological presentations. These are described in great detail, partly for the sake of beginning mentalists, and partly for the sake of magicians who may want to add one or several of these experiments to their repertoire. This book may thus well end up serving as an introduction to mentalism for them, hence the minutely detailed explanations. To the seasoned, veteran mentalists, I beg your indulgence.

THE LIAR

In the classic 'Living and Dead' test, one spectator writes the name of a deceased person and several others each write the name of a living person. The performer correctly identifies the dead person in some mundane, showy or eerie fashion. The premise of finding the one thing that's different from all the others in a group lends itself particularly well to a graphological presentation. In 'The Liar', several spectators write a true statement and one writes a lie; by analysing each handwriting, you find the lie.

The topic can be anything factual from the participants' personal or professional life, such as the name of their spouse or partner, best friend, pet, first love, mother's first name, employer, profession, make of car, what they had for lunch, city or street they live in, last holiday destination, and so on. If appropriate, it could be something relevant to the group, such as the geographical territory assigned to each person, when working for a roomful of salespeople. Or, if you like the James Biss style of presentation[9], the colour of underwear each person is wearing.

There are a number of methods for Living and Dead tests. Just about any method that involves several participants can be used here, although there's no point in using methods that use envelopes to prevent you from seeing what was written, since the whole point is for you to analyse the writing. One of the oldest and simplest of methods uses nothing more than an ordinary sheet of writing paper. Aside from being very simple and practical, it can also be done impromptu.

You tear the sheet into nine equal pieces; the lie is written on the slip that came from the centre of the sheet. You recognize it because it's the only slip that has four torn edges; all the others have at least one cut edge[10].

To do this as a regular part of your act, you can make it easier to fold the sheet evenly by putting pencil marks on all four edges of a stack of sheets, at ⅓ and ⅔ of each side, and fold the sheet across opposite marks. For impromptu performances, here's a quick way done all in the hands.

---

9   In his book, *Messing with Minds*.

10 The idea of using torn edges to locate the correct slip can be found, uncredited, in many old books, for example in the trick 'The quick or the dead' in T. Nelson Downs's *The Art of Magic*.

Hold the sheet with one hand in the middle of each long side and bring your hands together so that one is above the other. This creates an 'S'-shaped curve in the sheet. Adjust the position of the curves until they align with the edges, then carefully crease the paper, adjusting as you go. This divides the sheet into thirds quite evenly. Go over the folds with your fingernails to break the fibres.

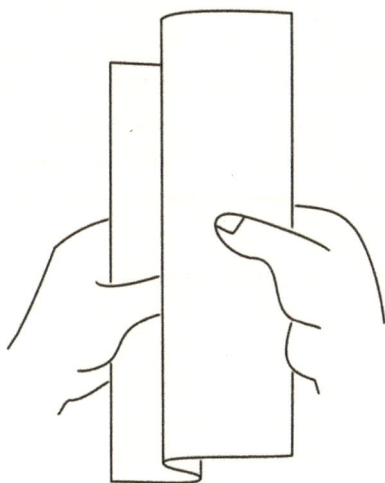

Open the sheet and do the same thing along the width. The sheet is now divided into nine sections. Open it again and tear off the first strip, along the long edge. Place it on the middle strip. Holding both the top and middle strips, tear again and place the first two strips on top of the third one. You now have the middle strip sandwiched between the two end strips.

Turn the stack of strips sideways, tear them and stack them exactly the same way. The slips are ready to be distributed; the key slip is in the middle of the stack, fifth from the top.

If you find it difficult to make the creases parallel, make them in two steps. Hold the sheet as above but at the upper corners, palms facing you so that you're looking down at the edge of the sheet. Proceed as above and make a crease on each side, near the top. Turn the sheet end for end, adjust the fold and make a crease on each side. Place the sheet on the table, crease both sides from end to end, then break the fibers as above.

If you perform this experiment impromptu, perhaps at someone's house, you may get a pad of paper that's perforated at the top. These don't always tear cleanly at the perforations, in which case the middle piece in the top row may have four torn edges as well. If the tear is irregular or at an angle, simply note this and proceed; you'll recognize this slip later on and know to ignore it. If, however, the tear is clean and straight, it's best to eliminate the slip from the experiment. You do this simply by turning over the stack before you hand out the slips and using no more than seven spectators. The tearing procedure leaves this slip second from the top; after you turn the stack over, it's eighth from the top. Nothing else changes: the fifth slip remains in fifth position.

To perform, get a sheet and tear it up as described. Distribute identical pens and the slips to the spectators; note who gets the fifth slip. It doesn't matter if there are fewer than nine spectators; as few as five will do, both for the method and for the effect you want to create.

"I need a person with an honest face to write a lie. That way, I can be sure that the lie is real... er, that the lie is a real lie. If you know what I mean... I'm not even sure that I know what I mean! Anyway—you have an honest face, so I'm going to ask you to be the one to write the lie." Make a big deal of carefully picking the right person to write the lie, eventually settling on the spectator who got the fifth slip.

Now explain what you want everybody to write. Have them write it as a full, but brief, sentence, e.g.: *"My partner is..."* or *"I ate ... this mor-*

ning", and so on. When they've finished writing, demonstrate or explain how to fold the slips—in half one way, then the other—so that everybody does it the same way. This is to make sure, you say, that all the slips look identical when folded.

Hand a glass to one of the participants in which to collect the folded slips. Have them mixed and the glass handed back to you.

Take a slip from the glass. *"Please don't tell me if I'm right or wrong"*. Open the slip and study it for a moment. If it's the slip with four torn edges, re-fold it and place it under the glass, saying that you'll get back to this one later. Otherwise, read out what's written on it, mention one or two character traits, claim that the statement is true and discard the slip. Do the same for the remaining slips.

Pick up the slip under the glass, open it and read out what it says. Mention a couple of traits, pause half a beat, then add that you also see a certain hesitation in the name or word, which betrays discomfort—and therefore, a probable lie. Address the participant: *"Is this yours?"* After she acknowledges that it is, thank her and take your bow. Discard the slips to prevent skeptical spectators from examining them afterward and possibly discovering the method used.

Sometimes you can actually spot a lie by looking closely at the writing. The offending word may be written a little differently from the rest of the text. Often, it will be surrounded by wider word spacing, as if the writer wanted to put some distance between herself and the lie.

PLAYING FAVOURITES

A 'Living and Dead' test can also be performed with a single participant. Although it can be presented as a lie detector test based on graphology, as in 'The Liar', it's far more interesting and impressive to present it as graphology combined with other knowledge. In this effect, you appear to determine a spectator's taste. You introduce a relevant topic; for example, music. The spectator writes the name of her favourite song as well as names of songs she doesn't particularly like. You eliminate the ones she doesn't like until you find the favourite.

Countless topics can be used. In addition to music, it could be books, authors, genres, historical figures, movies, television shows, actors, rock bands, cars, brands of beer or chocolate, foods, restaurants, flowers, travel destinations, hobbies, leisure activities, and so on. A topic relevant to the audience or the occasion is always welcome, of course.

Many methods for 'Living and Dead' tests work just as well with a single participant as with several. But when one person does all the writing, it makes more sense to have her write all the entries on a single sheet, rather than on individual slips of paper. An excellent method uses a standard, unlined index card, 7.5 x 12.5 cm (3 x 5 in), or a notepad of approximately the same size. The five or six entries are written one below the other, like a list.

To make it easy on a spectator who may not be very good at estimating, it's common to divide the card into six rows by writing the numbers 1 through 6, spread out evenly, in a single column near the left edge of the card, before handing it to the spectator. During the experiment, you instruct the spectator to write her selection next to any number she wants. She writes the other entries next to the remaining numbers, in any order.

Although the card has six rows, only five are used—one for the selection and four more for the indifferent entries. This gives the spectator a choice of where to write the last entry, instead of forcing her to put in the only available row. It's a tiny thing, but it helps create the impression of freedom of choice, which is psychologically sound.

The method is based on having the spectator write her selection first, before writing the names of the indifferent entries, and on the performer being able to recognize the first entry written. One way to accomplish this is by having the spectator write with a fairly soft pencil that has been sharpened to a very fine, tapering point. The first stroke written will be thinner than anything else on the card, because the sharp point soon gets dulled by writing[11] ('Cadillac' in the illustration.).

A ballpoint pen can also be prepared to make the initial stroke look different. Rubbing a tiny bit of wax or lip balm (e.g., ChapStick®) onto the tip makes it skip. Touching the tip of the pen to a stamp pad leaves a minuscule dot of a different colour. You can find very small ink pads, made for novelty rubber stamps or art projects, in many stationery, toy, and art supplies stores. Experiment with different supplies and ink colours until you find a combination that you can trust and spot.

---

11 Described, among other places, in 'The Quick and the Dead', *The Tarbell Course in Magic*, vol. 4.

```
1. Ford

2. Cadillac

3.

4. Nissan

5. Chevrolet

6. Rolls-Royce
```

When performing, you hand the pen to the spectator the moment you want her to start writing, no earlier. This gives her no time to toy with the pen and possibly test that it writes, which would destroy the preparation of the tip.

There may be times when it's a bit of a challenge to find the first entry written, perhaps because there's not enough light or the first stroke isn't as noticeable as you'd like it to be. But since you are now a bona fide graphologist in the eyes of the audience, you are perfectly entitled to get out your magnifying glass to get a better look at the handwriting—and to spot that initial stroke while you're at it. If you're concerned about a skeptical and astute spectator examining the card too closely after the performance and discovering the method, discard the card during or after the experiment.

To perform, select a spectator, preferably someone who wears glasses to ensure that she can see clearly. Introduce the topic if you're using a specific one, otherwise ask her about her leisure activities or preferred type of entertainment, and pick a suitable topic. When she names her choice—let's say it's rock music—tell her to think of one of her favourite songs. Instruct her to close her eyes and hear the song in her mind, as vividly as she can. Give her a few moments.

Hand her the pen and the card as you tell her to write the name of the song next to any number. When she's finished writing, have her show what she wrote to the spectators around her. Then tell her to think of a song that she does not like and to write it next to another number. Do this three more times.

Get the pen and the card back; put the pen away. Deliver a short reading on two or three traits as you study the handwriting. In the process, locate the favourite—the entry with the initial stroke.

"Now that I know a bit about you, I'm going to try to guess your taste in music." Appear to study the card briefly, then: *"You don't strike me as someone who would like..."*, and name any two non-favourites. Read out another non-favourite; appear to hesitate for a few moments, then face the participant and look for an unusual colour she may be wearing or, failing that, the most noticeable one. Ask her about it; for example: *"Do you always wear green?"* and wait for the answer. Appear pensive for a moment, then eliminate the entry. Read out the two remaining entries, the favourite and the last non-favourite. Make this appear more difficult than previously by taking more time, looking back and forth at the card and the participant, perhaps even mentioning, half to yourself, something about the colour and a trait from the earlier graphological analysis, e.g.: *"Hm, sociable and green, balance..."* (see 'Pentachrome', below, for the meaning of colours), hesitate some more, then announce the favourite. Have her acknowledge this and take your bow.

You can use any bit of 'psycho-babble'—fake psychology—that you like, instead of colour: facial expression, posture, even asking a question that seems to provide some psychological or neurological insight. Such questions can be humorous if you like, but they must sound reasonably plausible. A few examples are: *"When you're bored, do you prefer to daydream or to move around?"*, *"Do you prefer to sleep on your right side or on your left?"*, *"Do you dream in colour?"*, *"Do you prefer dogs or cats?"*, *"Does your desk or workspace look tidy or messy?"* and so on, as well as questions that relate directly to handwriting signs: *"Are you the life of the party or do you prefer to go unnoticed?"*, *"Do you prefer to be alone or around people?"*, and so on.

For certain occasions, the theme of relationships is more topical than that of favourites. There are special people in our lives, and then there are all the rest. The spectator writes a list of names from which you can accurately pick out the best friend from the mere acquaintances, the spouse from the neighbours, the family member from the strangers, and so on. You have the spectator form a strong mental image of the person, preferably one that involves more than one sense (*"Picture yourself talking to that person, hear the sound of his or her voice in your mind…"*). This gives you a strong basis for claiming that we write the names of those who are dear to us in a more vibrant way than the names of those to whom we are less attached.

Corinda's 'Living and Dead' test allows you to achieve virtually the same effect through the use of a nail writer instead of a prepared pen[12]. This method is also useful as an out in case you can't find the initial stroke. Not knowing which one is the favourite, you can't name the non-favourites, so you present the elimination procedure a bit differently. You speak as if to yourself and you don't read out the entries: *"No, not this one… or this one… this one, maybe…"* and so on.

To perform, have a pencil and a nail writer in your right jacket pocket. Follow the presentation as above until you've finished the elimination procedure. Take the pencil from your pocket as you say that you found the favourite and are going to put a check mark next to it. Pretend to put a check mark somewhere on the card, but hold the card vertically in front of your face and the pencil horizontally, so that it's impossible to tell exactly where you're writing.

Put the pencil away and get the nail writer on your thumb. Hold the card in readiness for nail-writing a check mark next to one of the entries and drop your arm to chest level. Ask the participant to name her favourite. Glance at the card, locate the entry, read it out and continue: *"… is indeed the one I picked as being your favourite"*, and write the check mark. Face the participant, pause briefly, then: *"Would you please verify that I put the check mark next to it?"*, show her the card, wait for her to acknowledge and take your bow.

---

12 In Corinda's *13 Steps to Mentalism*, which also contains an excellent treatise on nail-writing.

FORGERIES

'Forgeries' is simply a 'Living and Dead' test done with signatures. It looks much like 'Playing Favourites', but the method is entirely different. There is no secret: it's just pure observation. It doesn't require any special knowledge; anyone can do it with a bit of practice.

All you need is a piece of paper or index card, and a pen. These can be borrowed; you never have to touch them. For the convenience of the spectator, however, it's a good idea to divide the sheet into numbered rows, just as in 'Playing Favourites'.

Talk very briefly about signatures being a reflection of who we are and offer to do a demonstration. Give the spectator the pen and paper, turn away and instruct her to sign next to any number on the sheet. When that's done, ask her to make up a name and sign it in any of the remaining rows. Repeat this until there are four or five signatures on the sheet. Then take the sheet and reveal which signature is actually her own.

As discussed earlier, our signature is a very personal thing, a reflection of our inner self. This makes it very difficult for someone else to duplicate it, since that other person isn't us. Our signature contains some of the essence of who we are, which is something that nobody else has.

Signatures usually evolve over time. If you consciously decide to create a new one, it will slowly become your own, incorporating more and more of yourself as you use it. But at first, it will look and feel foreign, awkward. This is what you'll see when you look at the various signatures on the sheet. One will be written fluidly and have a natural, practiced look. The others are most likely to look carefully written or drawn, usually with uneven, rough or hesitant strokes.

That's all there is to it. With a bit of practice, you'll be able to find the real signature every time. If not, you can always resort to the out described above, or you can simply use the prepared pen, described in 'Playing Favourites', as a shortcut or as a fallback while learning.

Banachek describes almost exactly the same experiment[13]. He suggests going straight into asking the spectator to sign her name before you explain what the experiment is about, or even that it is an experi-

---

13 'Subtle Handwriting', in his book, *Psychological Subtleties.*

ment. This is to ensure that she signs without being self-conscious about her signature, and therefore, more fluidly.

FORGONE CONCLUSION

With little more than a different presentation, Corinda's 'Living and Dead' test becomes a unique prediction effect.

You need five to eight different objects, which can be anything from pictures of famous landmarks, to coloured marbles, to objects borrowed from the audience. As you borrow or introduce them, casually mention the word 'select' or equivalent in a sentence, for example: *"I selected these paintings specifically for this experiment"*, or *"I would like to borrow a few objects; show me what you have in your pockets or purse and I'll choose a few."*

Spread the objects out on the table in front of the participant: *"Please look at these for a few moments."* While she's looking at the objects, prepare an unlined index card by numbering it from one to the number of objects used. This ensures that she will write with the card in vertical (portrait) orientation, otherwise it may be difficult or awkward to nail-write the checkmark later on. Hand her the card and the pen and ask her to write down the name of each object next to the numbers, in any order.

Take the card and the pen; put the pen away. *"Give me a moment, please, while I make a note... done!"* Pretend to study the writing intently for a few moments, even using your magnifying glass if you carry one, then take the pencil from your pocket, pretend to write something on the card, replace the pencil, get the nail writer on your thumb and hold the card in readiness for nail-writing the check mark. Drop your arm to waist height or onto the table, keeping the back of the card and your fingers in view, or simply put the card on the table.

Address the participant as you gesture toward the objects. *"Now I would like you to think of one of these objects. You can go with your gut feeling, you can analyse each object before choosing one, you can pick one at random, it doesn't matter. Just let me know when you've decided on one."*

When she's ready, ask her to announce her choice. *"Can you explain how or why you picked the ...?"*, naming the selected object. Allow her to explain if she wants, then address the audience. *"Whenever we have to pick something, we look at the choices, think about them for a while, and then we make our decision. So decision-making is a conscious and logical process that takes a certain amount of time, as I'm sure you'll agree."* Scan the audience and wait for spectators to acknowledge.

"There's only one little problem with this: none of it is true." Pause briefly, then: *"We make most decisions subconsciously, not consciously... through emotions, not logic... and within the first four to five seconds, not after thinking about it."* Pause for a beat. *"This is why we are able to make snap decisions. When we bypass the reasoning process, we listen to the subconscious directly. We call it instinct, a hunch, a gut feeling, or intuition."* Pause for another beat. *"So why do we think it through before committing to a decision? To justify our choice to the conscious, logical mind. This helps assure us that we made the right decision."* Let this sink in[14].

Bring the card to eye level and find the location of the selected object. *"I was looking at your handwriting earlier and I noticed..."* and do a reading of two or three traits. Dominant zone, connectedness and originality fit best with the theme, but any traits will do. Face the participant and write the check mark as you ask: *"Do you know what this told me about what you would most likely pick?"* Wait for her to answer.

"Absolutely nothing!" Wait for the reaction, if any, to die down. Drop your arm again. *"I'll tell you what really happened. Maybe you remember: at the very beginning, I said something about having* selected *these* objects, then I asked you to look at them for several seconds. This influenced your subconscious to make a choice and gave it time to do so."* Pause for half a beat. Raise your hand so the card faces you: *"Then, when I looked at your handwriting, I found the item that you wrote with a bit more assurance than the others, and I put a check mark next to it. Do you see it next to your selection?"* Hand her the card and wait for her to acknowledge. *"So I knew what you were going to choose—even before you knew that you were going to choose anything at all!"* Take your bow.

Instead of a check mark, the prediction can be written on a small notepad. After studying the card, which doesn't have to be numbered in this variation, you put it away, then you pretend to write something on the notepad. Put the pencil away and get the nail writer in position. Nail-

---

14 This explanation is quite accurate, according to current psychological research. However, it is incomplete. Missing is the fact that we always have the option of making reasoned decisions as well.

write the name of the object while speaking, and for the climax, hand the notepad to another spectator to read out your prediction *"in a loud and clear voice"*.

This variation is particularly well suited to parlour and stage performances, for which you use larger objects, if appropriate (e.g., trade shows) or images of paintings, vacation destinations, leisure activities, and so on. For a fun version, use pictures of good-looking men (with pictures of women on the back, for a male participant). Print a name under each one, and have the participant decide which one she would date.

If it's appropriate and you make sure that nobody gets hurt or embarrassed, you can do it with men selected from the audience (never with women). Have each one write his name with a broad-tipped marker on a sheet of paper and hold the sheet in front of him, like a sign. If there are duplicate names, number them. After the preliminary, play it tongue in cheek and ask the participant to choose *"the gentleman you find most attractive—or the least unattractive"*. Don't ask her to explain her choice. Remind the audience that this is an experiment about decisions, then explain that we tend to find most attractive those who are most like us or, on the contrary, complete opposites. Continue by explaining how we make decisions and end as above.

You can perform the same effect with billets and an index. No nail writer is required, but you must know in advance all the possible choices. If you want to use borrowed objects, select six common, gender-neutral ones to guarantee that you can perform the effect for any audience: for example, a coin, keys, a pen, a watch, a card (any kind), and a piece of jewellery. Have all of these items with you as well, so you can add a missing one if necessary.

The most practical method for this is Larry Becker's ingenious use of a Himber wallet as an index15. You can use any type of Himber, z-fold, or other switching wallet. Write the name of each object on a small slip of paper, about 3 x 7.5 cm (1¼ x 3 inches). The exact size of the slips depends on the size of your wallet and its configuration; when the slips are folded in half twice, they should fit side by side into one pocket (or two pockets on the same panel) of the wallet. Insert the slips for half their length into the pocket in a memorized order; alternatively, write

---

15 In his book, *Stunners Plus*.

the order on a Post-it® note that you stick below the slips or on the facing panel. Close the wallet and open it to the other side. Insert a blank slip, similarly folded, into the matching pocket, also half protruding.

If the wallet is big enough, you can put a few index cards in another pocket, and if you use pictures rather than borrowed objects, you can put these in the wallet as well. Then you have a self-contained effect that you can carry and perform any time. Very inexpensive, plastic z-fold wallets are now available from magic dealers.

To perform, when it's time to write the prediction, open the wallet so that the audience sees that there's only one slip inside. Remove it, close the wallet, open the slip and hold it against the wallet, which you bring up to face level, the slip facing you. Pretend to write something, put the pen away, and refold the slip. Lower your hand, open the wallet so the inside is visible again, and put the slip back back where it was. Close the wallet and put it aside, ready to be opened to the index side.

To reveal the prediction, pick up the wallet and bring it to face level, open it and pull out the appropriate slip. As you pull it out, start closing the wallet, timing it so that half the slip is trapped inside the closed wallet and half protrudes from the top. Extend your arm toward the participant, asking her to remove the slip and read what you wrote. Finish as above, then casually pocket the slip; when you have a moment, put it back in its place in the index to reset for your next performance.

With a slightly different presentation, this experiment becomes a more traditional prediction effect. Select a topic that involves personal preferences (as described in 'Playing Favourites'). Start as above until after the participant has announced her choice. Instead of explaining how we make decisions, state that character traits often reveal a person's tastes, and that the participant's handwriting told you what she would most likely choose. Reveal the prediction and take your bow.

Art is a particularly interesting topic to use, if only because much research has been done in an attempt to link art preferences with personality types[16]. Get or make half a dozen cards (any size) of rather obscure paintings of very different styles, and print their name on the back. In

---

16 See, for example, http://www.bbc.co.uk/science/humanbody/mind/surveys/art/ as well as http://cocosci.berkeley.edu/annehsu/papers/premuzic-whoart.pdf

performance, introduce the cards with the writing side up, and don't turn them over until after you've written the prediction. This gives the experiment an air of authenticity and prevents the participant from reacting to the paintings, which could potentially ruin the effect by revealing her prefrence. It also prevents the audience from suspecting that you simply guessed what she would choose from her expression as she looked at the images.

QUASIMODAL

This effect is 'Playing Favourites' disguised as a book test of sorts. The name comes from the fact that the presentation revolves around the ways in which we store memories, which are sometimes called 'modes of representation[17]', hence 'modal'. The effect is exactly the same whether you use a prepared pen or a nail writer.

The description assumes the use of a small travel guide that covers a dozen or more European cities. Each city should have its own section or chapter. The book should be well illustrated with photographs of city scenes, rather than just tourist attractions.

"When I was a child, I found a travel guide, much like this one. I read it many times over; it made distant places come alive for me, and I dreamed of visiting them all." Slowly riffle through the pages, tacitly showing that they're all different. *"I would like to offer one of you a free trip to Europe—at least, a mental one. Who would like to go on this trip?"*

Select a volunteer. If you're working to a small group, you can add: *"Not only is it free, you don't even have to leave your seat!"* If you're bringing the participant up on stage, you can ask her if she had a good trip from her seat to the stage, joke about airline food, going through customs, and so on.

Hand her the book and face away from her. *"Please open the book to any page with a picture on it and look at the picture. If there are several, pick the biggest one. I'd like you to create a strong impression of the picture in your mind, so that you can remember it clearly later on."* Pause briefly, then continue, speaking slowly and pausing briefly between sentences: *"Notice the lines... the shapes... the colours.... Look at the picture*

---

17 Plus, it's a once-in-a-lifetime pun.

as a whole... now focus on a detail... and another one... and maybe one more." Pause briefly.

"Close your eyes if you wish, and imagine yourself stepping into the picture.... In your mind, hear the sounds that you'd expect to hear.... It could be the traffic on the street... conversations in a restaurant... or the hollow silence of a museum." Pause briefly.

"Now add physical sensations. Feel yourself standing, walking, sitting. Notice the air... smell the smells... feel the textures beneath your fingers. Now add the emotions... notice the feelings that come up from being in that scene... experience it fully, as if you were there." Pause for a few moments.

"Now open your eyes. At the top of the page, you'll see the name of the city you're in. Read it to yourself and remember it, then close the book and put it on the table." When she's done, face her, give her the pen and the card and instruct her to write the name of the city next to any number. Face away from her while she writes.

"Open the book to the table of contents at the front. Pick a different city and write its name next to any number you like. Keep doing this until the card is full." Turn away.

When she's finished writing, face her, get the pen and card back, and put the pen away. Study the writing, find the selection, and deliver the graphological reading, ending with the dominant zone. Pause briefly, then continue: *"People who, like yourself, are driven by instincts, often get the strongest impression from imagining physical sensations. Was this the case for you?"* For the upper zone, suggest that the strongest impression was either visual or auditory; for the middle zone, suggest emotions. This is actually a hit-or-miss proposition[18], but worth a try, since it's relevant to the presentation. If she agrees, take credit, otherwise simply acknowledge her answer (she may not know herself).

Study the card: *"I'm going to put a check mark next to the name of one city... there."* Put a check mark next to the selection and put the pen away. Ask her to name the city she has in mind. When she tells you, nod and continue: *"The place names you got from the table of contents look dull, flat, lifeless. But the place where the picture in your mind was taken looks more vibrant, more alive, and that is why I picked it."* Show her the

---

18 There doesn't seem to be any research attempting to correlate handwriting with modes of representation.

card: *"Do you see the check mark next to...?"* and name the city. After she acknowledges, take your bow.

Instead of a travel guide, you can use travel brochures, tourist information booklets or souvenir books. Many other kinds of illustrated books can be used as well, as long as they contain enough suitable photographs and have a layout and structure that fit the handling. There should be at least as many illustrated sections or chapters as there are numbers on the card (six is a good number), and the section name should appear on every page with a photograph. Although it is possible to work with individual captions instead of section names, the procedure becomes more cumbersome, so it's best avoided.

MURDER, THEY WROTE

A murder mystery for parlour or stage, loosely patterned after the popular Clue® (Cluedo® in the UK) game. It's essentially three instances of a 'Living and Dead' test, but disguised enough to hide the principle used.

On the table in front of you are: a notebook or notepad holder with an elastic strap closure; a stack of Jumbo size cards depicting suspects, rooms and weapons; a stack of fifteen slips of paper of three different colours—the top slip of each colour is marked; fifteen identical pens; a magnifying glass; a broad-tipped marker, black or blue; a clear bowl; a large manila envelope, and three smaller ones, the size of a card.

"I would like to read to you from the police notebook of Constable Copperpenny." Open the notebook and start reading. *"On the night of July 16, at 12:06 AM, an anonymous telephone call was received by the constabulary, saying that Sir Griswold Tiddleybotham had been murdered. Constable Pennyfarthing and I were dispatched to the scene, the Bedside Manor."* As an aside to the audience: *"Sir Tiddleybotham's grandfather had been a physician."*

"The murder had taken place after a dinner party. Most guests had left hours earlier. After interviewing those present, I determined that all had a grudge against Sir Griswold." As you describe each suspect (and later, the rooms and weapons), show the appropriate card, then pause briefly as you put the card down and pick up the next one. *"Sir Griswold's wife, Lady Gabriella Gabalot, had motive for murder. Sir Griswold had*

said that her new hat looked like last year's... lampshade. The French chef, Monsieur Escargot, had motive for murder. Sir Griswold had poured ketchup on his soufflé. The local newspaper's gossip columnist, Miss Hilary Hearsay, had motive for murder. Sir Griswold had said that even the canaries turned up their beaks at her column. Sir Griswold's artist niece, Miss Frieda Fresco, had motive for murder. Sir Griswold had said that her paintings looked like something his cat could have done... better. And finally, Sir Griswold's psychiatrist daughter, Dr. Vanessa Valium, had motive for murder. Sir Griswold had frequently remarked that it takes a crackpot to know one."

"While I was interviewing the suspects, Constable Pennyfarthing explored the mansion. He came across several rooms in which the dastardly deed could have taken place. The room for doubt. The room for improvement. The elbow room. The locked room. The whine cellar."

"Hidden in various parts of the mansion, Constable Pennyfarthing discovered several potential murder weapons. A badger, with which to badger the victim to death. A poison pen letter—death by poison. An icy stare, with which to freeze the victim to death. A chocolate cake—death by chocolate. And a glass of sorrows, in which to drown the victim."

"This left us with three questions. Who murdered Sir Griswold? Where did the murder take place? And what was the instrument of Sir Griswold's demise? Constable Pennyfarthing and I set out to find witnesses and clues."

Close the book, wrap the elastic closure around the front, and address the audience. *"This is where we come in, ladies and gentlemen. In a moment, I'm going to call on three members of the audience to play the role of witnesses. The witnesses are going to select the murderer, the room, and the weapon, and write their choices on slips of paper."* Pause briefly to allow the information to sink in.

"In addition to the witnesses, other members of the audience are going to write the names of the remaining suspects, rooms and weapons on slips of paper. These will serve as false leads to confuse the investigation—otherwise, we wouldn't have much of a mystery!" Smile and pause briefly.

"Then I will play the role of the detective and attempt to solve the case." While speaking, put the book on the table, the pens in your jacket pocket, and pick up the pile of cards, the smaller envelopes and the stack of slips.

Approach the first spectator of a group of five sitting next to each other and get her name—let's say it's Anna. Address the audience: *"Anna is go-*

ing to play our first witness, the one who saw the murderer." Give her the suspect cards, face down, and tell her to mix them a little, mimicking the action of mixing them at the fingertips. When she's finished mixing, give her an envelope, the first (marked) slip and a pen. Continue handing out pens and slips of paper of the same colour as you move from spectator to spectator. Tell the participants to simply hold onto the props for now. Repeat this procedure to set up two more witnesses—let's say that Bob selects the room and Carol selects the weapon—then return to the stage.

Address the audience, pausing between instructions: "*Now I'm going to ask the witnesses to make their choices. Look at the cards, select one and put it in the envelope…. Now pass the remaining cards to the people with pen and paper so that everybody gets a card—keep them printed side down, please, so that I can't see who gets what…. Everybody, please write the name of the card you're holding on the slip of paper…. Now fold the slip in half, side to side… and again, top to bottom*", mimicking the action with your hands. "*This way, all the slips look the same, so I'll have no way of knowing whose they are.*"

"*Now I'm going to collect everything, except the envelopes. These contain the evidence that will be used at the end of the investigation.*" Pick up the large manila envelope and hold it with its mouth open, so that participants can drop their cards into it without fumbling. Pick up the bowl with your other hand and approach the first witness. Have her drop her slip and pen into the bowl, and remind her that she is to retain her card in its envelope. Moving from participant to participant, collect the pens and slips in the bowl, and the remaining cards in the large envelope, which you hold at arm's length so that it's obvious that you can't see inside. When you've collected the props from the last participant, have her mix the slips while you hold the bowl. Collect the props from the two remaining groups in the same way, then return to the stage.

"*I would like to ask the three witnesses to please join me here on stage. Don't worry—nobody is going to be arrested or harmed in any way!*" Put the envelope and the bowl on the table, and put the pens aside.

Position the witnesses in the same order used throughout: murderer closest to you, then room, then weapon. Introduce the witnesses by name and ask the audience to applaud them. Hold up the bowl for all to see and address the audience: "*These are the names of all the suspects, rooms and weapons. Three of these are actual clues: the ones written by our three witnesses. The others are merely false leads."* Pause to let this sink in. *"I'm going to play the role of the detective—or, more accurately, the Psychological Sleuth. To solve the case, I have to find the suspect Anna picked, the room Bob picked, and the weapon Carol picked."*

"Anna, I would like you to think of the suspect you chose. If you like, you can have a peek at the card in the envelope to refresh your memory. I'll turn away in the mean time." Dump the slips onto the table and put the bowl down. Pick out the suspect slips—you can find them very quickly thanks to the colour-coding—open them and stack them in your hand, writing side up. This gives you ample opportunity to find the marked slip. Memorize it or dig your thumbnail into a corner of the slip so that you can recognize it easily later. Ask the witness if she's ready, tell her to make sure you can't see the card, then turn to half-face her.

"Turn a little bit toward me, please... thank you. I'm going to read out the names of all the suspects. Please don't say or do anything while I do this—just concentrate on the name of the suspect you chose and look at me. I'm going to try to determine from your expression which one you selected." Read to yourself the name on the first slip, then look up at the witness and call out the name as you appear to study her face. Pause very briefly, then move the front slip to the back of the stack. Repeat this for the four remaining slips, at a fairly brisk pace.

"Micro-movements in the face are very difficult to spot, because they can last as little as one fifteenth of a second. I think I caught one, but I'd like to try this again, just to be sure." Repeat the sequence, then announce that you now know who the murderer is. Mix up the slips and approach the table. Making sure that no one can see the writing, go through the slips one by one, crumpling up the unmarked ones and tossing them in the bowl. Flatten the remaining, marked slip if necessary. Pick up the notebook and slide the end of the slip under the elastic closure, near the top of the notebook. Replace the notebook on the table, slip side down.

"Bob, I would like you to concentrate on the room you chose. Feel free to have a peek at the card to refresh your memory while I get the slips of paper ready." Pick out and prepare the appropriate slips as above, then face the witness. *"I'm not going to study your face, Bob; instead, I'm going to ask you to repeat what I say. Ready?"* When he acknowledges, face the audience and read the slip as a sentence: *"I chose the room for doubt"*,

for example. The witness repeats this. Pause very briefly, as if reflecting, then move the front slip to the back of the stack. Repeat until you've gone through all the slips.

To the audience: "*That was easy! Changes in voice pattern are much more noticeable. With a bit of practice, you can easily hear differences in pitch, response time, hesitation, etc. Perhaps some of you noticed slight changes in Bob's voice.*" Mix the slips as you approach the table, crumple up the four unmarked ones and drop them into the bowl. Flatten the marked slip if necessary and slide it under the notebook's closure, below the first slip. Place the notebook on the table, slip side down.

"*Carol, instead of analysing your reactions, I'm going to ask you a few questions about yourself so that I can get to know you a little bit. I will try to find the handwriting that matches your character traits.*" Questions are necessary here to prove that you cannot identify the writer from the handwriting alone, otherwise the audience may wonder why you bothered with body language and voice patterns when a glance at the slips would have sufficed. For the same reason, and also to avoid lessening the suspense, it's best to avoid performing other experiments that use graphology in the same act.

Open and stack the remaining five slips. Appear to study them for a few moments, occasionally using the magnifying glass and glancing at the spectator. Eventually take one of the unmarked slips, crumple it up and toss it in the bowl as you say: "*I can tell that you didn't write this; it doesn't match what I get from your posture and body language.*"

Now you ask the questions as you appear to study the slips some more. You can ask psycho-babble questions, graphology-related questions, such as: "*Do you prefer to go out with friends or stay home?*", "*Do you like to be the centre of attention at parties?*", "*Are you detail-minded or do you usually see the 'big picture'?*", and so on, or a combination of both. After each question, acknowledge her answer and eliminate an unmarked slip. When you're down to the last one, hold it up and address the audience, brightly: "*Got it!*" Slide the slip under the notebook's closure, below the first two slips.

"*I have finished my investigation. I believe that these are the clues that solve the case—the murderer that Anne chose, the room that Bob chose, and the weapon that Carol chose—and that these are the false leads.*" As you say this, first hold up the notebook and point to each slip in turn,

135

then lower the notebook and hold up the bowl for a moment. Put it back on the table and announce: *"And now, ladies and gentlemen, the moment of truth!"* Hold the notebook at shoulder height, slips toward the audience, then dramatically call out the three clues, pointing to each slip in turn and pausing ever so slightly between clues, e.g.: *"It was Miss Hilary Hearsay. In the elbow room. With a glass of sorrows."*

Pick up and uncap the marker. *"Anna, please pull your card out of the envelope and show it to the audience. Does it say Miss Hilary Hearsay?"* After she acknowledges, look at her card, as if to verify her answer for yourself, then put a large check mark on the slip and announce: *"Correct!"* Repeat this procedure with the two remaining witnesses.

Cap the marker and put it on the table, together with the notebook. To the audience: *"And there you have it, ladies and gentlemen. The murder of Sir Griswold Tiddlybotham has now been solved. We have established beyond doubt that it was..."* Collect the cards from the witnesses: *"... Miss Hilary Hearsay... in the elbow room... with a glass of sorrows."* Put the cards on the table and address the audience as well as the witnesses: *"The case is now closed. I have it on good authority that the murderer was arrested, tried, found guilty and sentenced to life in prison. But, with good behaviour, the sentence was reduced to 200 years."* To the audience, gesturing in the appropriate direction: *"Please give all the participants a big hand: the members of the audience who provided the false leads... the witnesses..."*, whom you thank and send back to their seats, *"and... the Psychological Sleuth!"* Smile and take your bow.

The background story can be adapted to any period, setting, and style of humour. It can also be shortened by presenting the facts without the policeman's narrative and the suspects's motives. Then there's less need for humour, so the suspects, rooms and weapons can be ordinary.

The notebook can be replaced by a notepad holder in which you can store most of the props. An inner pocket can hold a few sets of slips. The small envelopes and the large one, with the cards inside, can go on top of the notepad. A separate elastic strap closure, available in stationery stores and wrapped around the closed holder, keeps everything together.

The slips only have to be small enough for three of them to fit comfortably on the notebook or notepad holder. To mark them, a nail nick will do. You can put one in ahead of time, or as you hand out the slips.

The cards have the name of the suspect, room or weapon at the bottom, and a simple illustration at the top. These only have to be symbolic for the rooms and weapons, e.g.: a key for the locked room, an 'A+' for improvement, a question mark for doubt, a pair of angry eyes shooting icicles for the icy stare, eyes shedding tears into a glass for the glass of sorrows, and so on. The lettering and illustration styles should match the setting and period of the story.

The most expedient way to make the cards is to print them on a laser or inkjet printer on thick card stock, cut them to size and seal them in laminating pouches. These should preferably be matte, to avoid glare when the witnesses show them to the audience, and fairly thick, for rigidity. The cards can be printed on coloured stock to match the colours of the slips. The exact dimensions of the cards depend upon the size of the laminating pouches, which also determine the size of the small envelopes.

For an interesting and effective variation, you have the participants make up their own suspects, rooms and weapons, rather than presenting them with ready-made ones. There is thus no need for a story nor for cards. You can give the participants the freedom to choose any person or character, location, and method of killing of their choice, or you can provide a theme that suits the audience or the occasion, from comic books to Russian literature. The only restriction is that there should be no duplicate choices.

The procedure is generally the same until the revelation. After you announce *"the moment of truth"*, you approach the first witness, holding the notebook so that she can't see the slips, and tell her to name out loud the suspect she has in her mind. Turn the notebook toward her, point to the first slip and have her read it out. State that you are correct and put a checkmark on the slip. Do the same with the two other witnesses, then announce that the mystery has been solved and call out the three clues as above, e.g.: *"It was Robinson Crusoe. On Mars. With a garden gnome."* You'll often find funny combinations that you can milk. Finish as above.

Finally, you can perform this version virtually impromptu. You only need three pens, which are passed from participant to participant within each group, and three sheets of paper. Fold a sheet in half down the length, tear, stack the two strips, then fold them into thirds, as described in 'The Liar'. Unfold the strips, tear them and place the end pieces on top of the middle pieces. Count five slips from hand to hand, reversing their order, and discard the last slip. Now the slips can be distributed, the top one going to the witness. It's the only slip with a single cut edge; the remaining ones have two.

After the participants have written down their choices, the witnesses collect the pen and the slips from their group. They hand you the slips as you need them. Everything else is as above, except that, at the end, you hold the slips in your hand instead of on the notebook.

PENTACHROME

In the classic mentalism experiment, 'Pseudo Psychometry[19]', the performer accurately describes and finds the owner of each of a number of borrowed objects, even though his back is turned to the audience while the objects are collected. 'Pseudo Psychometry' is a very powerful effect—so strong, in fact, that it's often used to close a mentalism act. It's no wonder, then, that so many versions and variations of the experiment exist, both in print and as dealer items.

'Pentachrome' is a version of 'Pseudo Psychometry' that revolves around character analysis[20]. It incorporates a Lie Detector effect and a divination[21]. The name is a combination of the Greek words for 'five' and 'colour'. Five is a practical number of spectators to use, but you can do it for ten or more, and the presentation involves a colour test.

You hand a business card and a pen to each of five participants. You ask four spectators to write down the name of their favourite colour, and one spectator, which you designate, to write the name of a colour she dislikes. When they've all finished writing, they leave their cards on the

---

19 Although 'Pseudo Psychometry' will forever be linked with Theo. Annemann, he actually only claimed credit for the method. The general effect goes back to mediumistic stunts of the 19th century. Annemann's method is used in one form or other in virtually every version of the effect, including the one described here.

20 L. Vosburgh Lyons seems to have been the first to apply 'Pseudo Psychometry' to handwriting. See 'Graphology', *The Jinx*, no. 74 (also in Annemann's *Practical Mental Effects*). It remains a stellar routine for stage and is well worth studying.

21 'Pentachrome', although devised independently by the author, is very similar to Phil Goldstein's 'Desire', in *The Blue Book of Mentalism*, and to Larry Becker's 'Sneak Thief', in his book *Stunners*.

table, writing side down. You look away during all this, explaining that you don't want to be influenced by what you might see.

The cards are gathered, mixed and handed to you. You show the first card around, explain what the choice of colour means, then continue with a brief graphological reading, pointing out how the meaning of the colour and the signs in the handwriting complement each other.

After studying the spectators in silence and a moment of hesitation, you hand the card to one of them. "*This is yours, I believe.*" The spectator acknowledges that you are correct.

You pick up the next card and do exactly the same thing as for the first. For the third card, you do the readings but notice a hesitation in the writing. "*No need to figure out who wrote this one*", you say as you hand the card to the spectator who was asked to write a colour she dislikes. She acknowledges that it's hers.

You deal with the fourth card as for the first two. The last card stays on the table, writing side down. You ask the remaining participant a psycho-babble question or two, as described in 'Playing Favourites', above. Then you deliver a reading for her, and end by naming the colour that you think she is most likely to chose. This is verified to be correct.

You bow and exit. There's very little you can do to top that.

The methods are very simple. The cards are secretly numbered and handed out in sequence, starting, say, with the spectator on the far left and moving toward the right, one person at a time. The first spectator thus gets card number one, the next gets card number two, and so on. Later, when the cards are handed to you, you can tell at a glance the value of any card by reading the secret marking, which tells you the position of the spectator you gave it to, counting from the left again. So, for example, if you look at a card and see that its value is four, then you know that you gave that card to the fourth spectator from the left.

To determine the disliked colour, you remember the number of the card you give to the spectator that you designate to write it. To name the colour at the end, you secretly get a glimpse of the writing beforehand.

There are several ways to mark the cards. For impromptu demonstrations, the cards can be lightly nail-nicked along one long edge, either beforehand or while you're distributing them. With the cards all facing the same way, nick each one at a different location, as evenly spaced as possible. The position of the nick gives you the card's value, going from left to right when the cards are printed side up. You can mark and decipher up to five cards easily this way. For more than that, an additional nick on one short edge allows you to code the numbers six to ten, two nicks gives you eleven to fifteen, and so on.

Here's a way to nail-nick five cards quickly and accurately[22]. Hold a packet of cards, printing side down and top of the printing to the right, in your left hand. Deal five cards into your right hand, one below the other and each one injogged by about 12 mm (½ inch)—you can use your extended left little finger as a gauge. Once the cards are positioned, simply dig your right thumbnail into the edge, about 12–18 mm (½– ¾ inch) above the bottom edge of the top card, as illustrated. The action can be covered by turning the body, by rotating the hand inward, by shielding the cards with the left hand as it comes over to square the cards, and so on. Square the cards and distribute them; the top card is number one, the next is two, and so on.

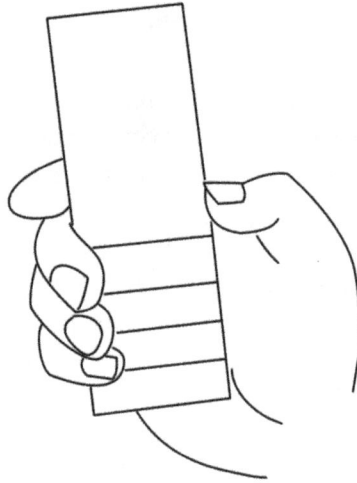

The nick has to be as small as possible. You'll have to practice to feel how much pressure is enough and how much is too much. If your thumbnail is very short, you'll need to apply greater pressure than if it's long. Alternatively, you can scratch the cards, rather than nick them, by bending your thumb inward after it's in position against the edges.

---

22 Devised by the author.

When working with nail-nicked cards, it's wise to remove the nick before handing the card back. This is done by dragging the card between your thumbnail on one side and fingernails on the other while casually toying with the card. You do this without looking, when you address the audience or a particular spectator.

Another way to mark cards is with a soft pencil. The marks go on one long edge, just like the nail nicks. With this method, you can mark up to ten cards and still be able to read the number with little effort. You do this by dividing the card in half visually; this gives you the numbers one to five on the left, six to ten on the right. If that's not enough to give you the number, visually divide the appropriate half in half again. The halfway marks are at three on the left and eight on the right. Now you only have to count one or two position in the appropriate direction and you'll have the number. With some practice, you'll soon do this automatically, but if you still have trouble reading the value, try coding eight cards, rather than ten.

Cards can also be marked on the printed side, rather than on the edge. With a soft pencil, you can add some subtle shading to the loops of different letters across a line. Alternatively, you can make tiny scratches through the ink with the tip of a craft knife (e.g., X-ACTO®) or a needle.

The most efficient way is to have the marks printed as part of the card's design. Then you don't have to spend any time marking cards before a show. You can make these yourself: good-looking business card stock is available from stationery and office supply stores. There are ten cards to a sheet, so you can have either two sets numbered from one to five, or one set numbered from one to ten.

A very practical and expedient way to code the cards is to have the actual number hidden in some other piece of information. For example, you can change the last- or next-to-last digit of your postal code; it may slow down mail delivery a bit but won't stop it from coming through. Besides, you're more likely to be contacted by telephone or over the internet these days, so the postal address is less important—and if it is, you can always have an additional, unprepared business card that you keep separate from the coded ones. Another approach is to hide the code number in some made-up piece of information, such as a membership number or a business or permit number—or even the year you won a certain imaginary prize!

There are also ways to code the values into the text of the card without using numbers. For example, you can play with variations in the punctuation and other marks, in your logo or other image, or in a tag line. Let's say that your card announces 'Handwriting Analysis', and let's say that, to create a certain look, you have those words set in four or five different typefaces, 'ransom note' style. You can then use a distinctive typeface exclusively to encode the value. For example, you use *Comic Sans* only for the 'H' on card number one, only for the 'a' on card number two, only for the 'n' on card number three, and so on. Then you only have to spot the one letter that's printed in *Comic Sans* to you know the value of the card.

One final way is to encode the value in some kind of graphical border, using essentially the same system as for edge markings. Let's say that your card has a border of tiny diamond shapes all around, with solid ones alternating with hollow ones. One of the hollow diamonds at the top of the card can have a tiny dot in the middle. The position of the dotted diamond in the row tells you the value of the card. Instead of a dot, you could have some kind of imperfection, a slightly bolder outline, and so on.

When you hand out the cards, you do so from left to right or right to left, or alternating sides of the aisle, or every second person in the front row, or any other easily remembered sequence that suits the seating arrangements.

In general, it's best to number printed cards up to five (or six if you prefer), rather than up to ten or twelve. Should you need more than five cards during a performance, you can code additional sets with nail nicks. Let's say that your cards are coded up to five, and you find yourself working at a table for twelve, as can be the case in banquet halls. Hand out the first five cards as usual, add a nail nick to the next five, and two nail nicks to the last two. When reading the cards, add five to the coded number for every nick to get the actual value.

It's a good idea to devise a strategy for handling unused cards from a set, either because you had to use additional cards, as mentioned earlier, or because you performed for fewer than five people. One approach is to move the remaining cards to the bottom of the stack, below some kind of separator card that you always keep there. After the show, discard the extra cards or find a way to use them (perhaps with a nail nick), and reset your stack.

If you print your cards yourself, you can number them according to the venue, which is a useful consideration when working banquets, for instance. Although there are tables that seat five people, the most common numbers are six, eight, ten and twelve—even numbers, to accomodate couples. It's worth asking about seating arrangements ahead of time.

Whichever marking system you decide to use, make sure that the coding is subtle, in case spectators get suspicious and decide to compare their cards. Alternatively, discard the cards at the end of the experiment instead of handing them out.

Any of these encoding methods can also be used for business card tick sheets. The miniature tick sheet gives you extra opportunities for encoding. For example, if each trait is preceded by a check box, you can make a different one bolder on each card of your set. If each trait is numbered and followed by a period, such as '1.', you can use a bolder period. For teaser cards, you could have a thin line of diamond shapes or circles in the middle of the card to separate the tick sheet from your contact information. The line can be used to encode values, as described above. The same can be done with a design in the middle of the card: e.g., a border around the question mark in the illustration.

Note that the handlings given in this section assume that the cards are coded on the printed side. If you use cards that are coded on the edge—with nail nicks or pencil marks—you can often simplify one step or eliminate it completely, since these markings can be read from either side of the card.

To perform, distribute the pens—which should all be identical—and the cards, but take the trouble to orient the cards properly. Even though you hand them out with the printed side down, the printing should be right-side up for the spectator if she could see through the card. This increases the likelihood that the writing will be oriented the same way as the printing, which gives you a point of reference. When you do the glimpse later on, you'll know which way to hold the card so that you can read the writing right-side up. No guarantees, of course; the spectator may turn the card before writing on it, in which case you'll have to read it upside-down. But that's not too difficult.

"I'd like to ask all of you to please think of your favourite colour—except you. I'd like you to think of a colour that you particularly dislike." You can either choose the spectator and memorize her card's number, or you

can decide to always pick the spectator who gets card number four, for example, to think of a disliked colour.

Explain that you don't want to see what anybody wrote and turn away. Have a spectator gather the cards, mix them and hand them to you, writing side down, when everybody has finished writing.

When you receive the stack, recap what has happened as you deal the cards from hand to hand, rotating them in the horizontal plane as needed so that the printing faces the same way on each card, and also positioning the card with the disliked colour third from the top. End by holding the packet in dealing position, with the ball of the thumb at the outer left corner and the top of the printing toward the fingers. Note and memorize the value of the top card or remember the spectator at that number, whichever is easier for you.

Address the audience with a question or a humorous remark, e.g.: *"Do you all remember what you wrote?"* or *"I hope nobody wrote 'chartreuse' or 'fuchsia'—are those even colours or are they air freshener scents?"* While the spectators react, continue looking at them. Rotate your left wrist slightly inward, toward yourself, and with your right hand, grasp the top card from the front end and turn it over toward you, replacing it on top of the packet. Although you're not trying to hide what you're doing, this handling helps gives the impression that you turned the whole packet over, rather than just the top card, in case an astute spectator tries to reconstruct the trick later on. Drop your right hand and tilt your left hand forward so that the cards are horizontal again.

Once the reaction has died down, openly glance at the top card. If the writing is upside-down, rotate the card horizontally so that the top of the writing is near your fingers. Address the audience: *"I'll show you the card; just notice what's written on it and remain neutral."* As you say the second part, turn your head toward the spectator on the far right, look in the direction of her eyes, raise your left hand to eye level as you turn it palm outward, and extend your thumb. While she sees the top card, you get a glimpse of the writing on the bottom card, visible between your thumb and first finger[23]. Read and memorize the name of the colour written on it, and also burn the image of the writing into your mind. Re-

---

23 This glimpse is from Patrik Kuffs's 'Bold Business', on his DVD, *Mind Stunts I*.

member whatever signs you can: at the very least, slant and size. These are easy to determine at a glance, even if the writing is upside-down.

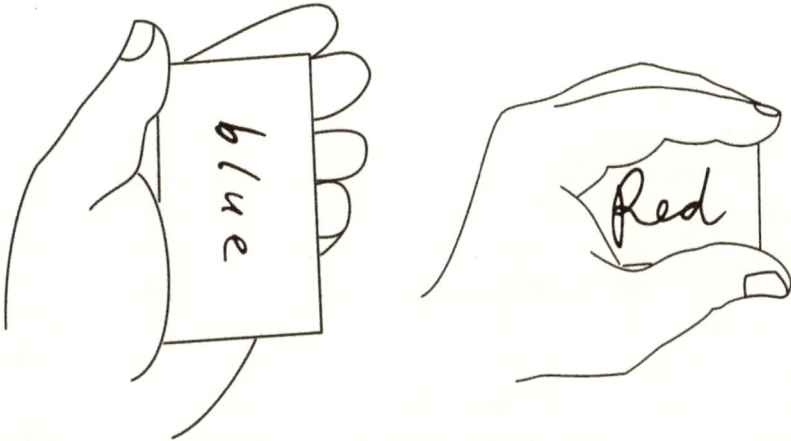

Without pausing, move your arm to the left in a sweeping motion, not too fast, so that every spectator can see the writing on the top card. Your gaze follows your hand. After you've shown the card to the spectator on the far left, lower your thumb, turn your left hand palm up and drop it to about waist level. The cards should be more or less horizontal again.

Address the audience: "*Our choices tell us something about us. The colour...*", bring your right hand over toward your left hand, take the top card with your right, move your right hand up to about the level of your right shoulder, look at the card and read out the name of the colour. As you do so, place the packet on the table, somewhat to your left, printing side up. Without pausing, continue with the appropriate reading for the named colour, as given below. Address the audience as you're doing this, and if the cards are coded with nicks, now is a good time to remove them.

White: "*People who like white are serene and enlightened. They strive for excellence, simplicity, recognition. They are seen as sweet and innocent.*"

Yellow: "*People who like yellow are optimistic, energetic and creative. They have high ideals. They are warm and cheerful.*"

Brown: "*People who like brown are stable, reliable and conscientious. They love hearth and home. They have strong values and take life seriously.*"

Orange: "*People who like orange are energetic, cheerful and playful. They like structure and organization. They are very sociable.*"

Red: *"People who like red are dynamic, courageous and constantly active. They live life to the fullest. They are very passionate in everything they do."*

Pink: *"People who like pink have a strong personality and a sensitive heart. They are caring and sharing. They are very affectionate, caring and nurturing to others."*

Purple: *"People who like purple are sensitive, observant and have deep feelings. They are creative and artistic. They have a complex personality."*

Blue: *"People who like blue are calm, sensitive and committed. They like harmony and tranquility. They make loyal and trustworthy friends."*

Teal: *"People who like teal are sensitive and stable, and have excellent taste. They march to the beat of their own drummer. They are very trusting."*

Green: *"People who like green are moral, persistent and calm. They like security, balance and stability. They are affectionate."*

Grey: *"People who like grey are practical, solid and articulate. They work very hard and are dedicated to their commitments. They are seen as very responsible."*

Black: *"People who like black have authority and power. They like sophistication. They are highly respected by others."*

You can shorten these readings to two sentences or even one. Let the colour reading sink in for a moment, then do the graphology reading. Let this sink in, then scan the participants for a few moments, hesitate appropriately, then squarely face the spectator whose number corresponds to the card you're holding. *"This, I believe, is yours"*, you say as you hand the card to her. *"Correct?"* The spectator acknowledges. Smile and let this sink in for a moment before continuing.

Pick up the top card from the packet on the table. Show the writing to the spectators in exactly the same, sweeping motion, then do the readings as above. End by handing the card to its owner. The next card, the third, is the one with the disliked colour. Proceed as for the previous two cards, but end by saying: *"But I detect some hesitation in the writing, so it's probably not really a favourite colour, which means that it was written by... you!"* Hand the card to the appropriate spectator.

Handle the next card the way you did the first two. There will be one card left on the table. Glance at it, but don't touch it. Appear deep in thought for a moment, then announce, perhaps in an overly dramatic and pompous tone, whom it belongs to. This should get a few groans and snickers, since there's only one spectator left. Wait for the reaction to die down before continuing.

"*Since there's no point in trying to determine who wrote on this card, I'm going to do the opposite: find out who you are.*" Now you're going to spend a few moments apparently doing a very quick psychological evaluation by asking a few questions. If you can pick up something in the spectator's posture or notice a mannerism that isn't embarrassing to mention in public, ask her about it: "*Do you always lean to the left?*", "*Do you often cross your arms?*", and so on. Also ask her a psycho-babble question or two, as described earlier. Do this rather quickly, and if you like, end with a humorous question—without necessarily waiting for an answer—which you then acknowledge as having nothing to do with the analysis; for example: "*Do you like my suit?*", "*Why is the sky blue?*", and so on.

Now deliver the reading, based on every sign you can remember from the signature, as well as the traits associated with the chosen colour. Let this sink in for a moment, then end with: "*From that, I would guess that your favourite colour is...*" and name the colour. Immediately pick up the card and show the writing to the audience, then look at it yourself, nod to acknowledge that you got it right and take your bow.

Other presentations are possible. For the effect to make sense in the context of mentalism presented as psychology, the topic should be either favourites or a psychological test. In the audience's view, this guarantees that you know all the possible answers and could, therefore, conceivably guess a particular spectator's choice. However, being able to guess the name of a pet, for example, just isn't believable. Unless the pet is dead and you claim to be psychic.

The kinds of tests you would use for this experiment are generally limited to specific choices or categories, but for favourites, you have to impose restrictions. For example, if you ask spectators to write the name of their favourite fruit, make it clear that it should be a common one. Otherwise, you may be in the uncomfortable position of having to convince the audience that the spectator couldn't *possibly* have picked anything but a sapodilla. Not so good.

A quick search on the internet for 'personality quiz' or 'personality test' will yield dozens of tests you can use. A fun one is 'Ice Cream Flavorology', which is based on a study commissioned by US ice cream manufacturers to find links between favourite flavour of ice cream and personality traits. As the humorist Dave Barry would say: I am not making this up.

Vanilla: *"You are impulsive, expressive and idealistic."*
Chocolate: *"You are lively, creative, the life of the party."*
Butter pecan: *"You are orderly, perfectionistic and detail-oriented."*
Banana: *"You are easy-going and generous."*
Strawberry: *"You are skeptical and reserved."*
Chocolate chip: *"You are ambitious and charming in social situations."*

After the ice cream reading, you do the graphology reading as usual.

You can, of course, make up your own tests and interpretations. Make the interpretations humorous, or with both a humorous and a serious interpretation, and you'll have a very entertaining routine.

AUTHENTICATION

A simpler and slightly shorter version of 'Pentachrome' with a 'Lie Detector' theme.

"If you watch television, maybe you've seen those experts who can tell when someone is lying. I'd like to try an experiment in lie detection." Hand out pens and marked business cards in order, blank side up.

Turn away from the participants. *"I'm going to ask each of you to write the word 'lying'—L-Y-I-N-G—on your card, then turn the card writing side down on the table."* Words like 'lying' and 'honesty' are topical, but you can use any word you like, or even give the participants a choice of words. After they've finished writing, continue, with appropriate gestures: *"In a moment, I'm going to turn away. When I do, I would like some of you to keep your card, and I would like the others to exchange cards, so that you're holding someone else's card. Ok?"* When they've nodded, turn away and continue: *"Go ahead, please do that now."* Give them a few moments, then: *"So, some of you have your own card, and some of you have someone else's card. Is this correct?"* Wait for acknowledgement, then add: *"Everybody, please put your card on the table in front of you, writing side down."*

Turn back to face the participants, approach the table and slide the cards toward yourself in a row. *"In a moment, I'm going to show each of you your card and ask if you wrote it. Whether you did or didn't, I would like you to answer 'yes'.*" Look at all the participants and nod in a slow, exaggerated motion when you say "yes", to help the idea sink in.

As you pick up the first card, note and remember its coded number. Hold it up so that the writing faces the first spectator, without you being able to see it, and ask, *"Did you write this?"* and nod again as you look the participant in the eye. The spectator should say *"Yes"*; if she doesn't, repeat the instructions and the question. Look at her while she answers, then pause briefly, as if analysing her response; finally, announce your verdict. If the coded value corresponds to her position, say: *"Yes, you wrote this"*, and place the card on the table in front of her, writing side up. If it doesn't, say: *"No, you didn't write this"*, and put the card to the side, away from the spectators and writing side down, in what will become a discard pile.

Go through the remaining cards in the same way. When done, look at the participants and make a sweeping gesture toward their cards: *"Did I correctly identify the truth from the lies?"*, ending by pointing at the discard pile. After they acknowledge that you did, thank the participants and allow the reaction to die down.

Slide the discards toward the nearest spectator and ask her to mix them up. *"It's easy when people tell the truth, but what if they don't? ... Then you have to find another way."* Take the cards back and hold them writing side up. *"Please don't give me any indication as to whom each card belongs to."*

Show the writing on the face card to the audience, then study it briefly and give a one- or two-point reading. When done, turn the top card over so it's writing side down, and place it on the bottom of the packet. Go through the remaining cards the same way. There will be either two, three or four cards in the packet.

"Now let's see...." Look at the audience as you mix the cards briefly, keeping them writing side down at all times. Hold the packet in one hand, writing side down, and hand the cards out to their respective owners, in quick succession, as follows: glance down to get the value of the top card, take it with your other hand, glance at the writing so that only you can see it, then hand the card to its owner. *"I believe this is your writing... and this is yours... "*, and so on.

"Is this correct?" After they acknowledge that it is, take your bow.

ULTROMETRY

A somewhat pretentious name for the 'Forgeries' experiment, performed with several spectators and a 'Pseudo Psychometry' ending. Each participant writes his or her signature as well as several made-up ones on a card. The cards are collected and you find the genuine signatures. You end by returning each card to its writer.

Divide five or six index cards into numbered rows, as described in Forgeries, but introduce small variations from card to card so that they're secretly marked as for Pentachrome. For example, you can slightly embolden the period after the '1' on the first card, after the '2' on the second, and so on, or place it just a tiny bit closer to—or farther from—the numeral.

Hand out the cards in order and perform 'Forgeries' as described, turning away while the participants are writing. As in 'Pentachrome', a spectator collects the cards, mixes them and hands them to you.

Pick up a card, cross out the fake signatures and circle or otherwise mark the genuine one. Show the card to all the participants, but tell them not to let you know, in any way, whose card it is nor whether you're right or wrong. When all the spectators have seen the card, put it on the table in front of you, writing side down.

Do the same for the remaining cards. When you're done, address the participants. "*Without giving me any details: how did I do?*" Even if you got one or two wrong, it's still a very impressive effect. Regardless of the answer, acknowledge it and continue: "*Let me see if I can do better.*"

Pick up the cards and turn them writing side up. For a few moments, pretend to study them intently, glance at the participants once in a while, and rearrange the order of the cards, eventually putting them in the order of the secret markings. Square the cards, then quickly put each one on the table, writing side up and properly oriented, in front of its respective owner. "*Yours. Yours. Yours. Yours. And yours.*" Let this sink in for a moment, then add: "*Correct?*" After they acknowledge, take your bow.

If you hand out prepared pens or pencils, as in 'Playing Favourites', you can always spot the correct signature. This also allows you to use any topic you want, not just signatures. The drawback is that you have to carry many pens or pencils, or spend a fair bit of time resetting, if you're working for more than one table at an event.

If you perform this experiment often, it's worth your while to print the cards, rather than number them by hand. Card stock, either full sheets that you cut yourself or pre-perforated to index-card size, is available in stationery and office supply stores. You can easily make bolder dots or introduce some variation or imperfection in the digits themselves to create the secret markings. You can use the back of the cards for contact and marketing information, just like the postcard-size tick sheet described earlier.

PENDULARITY

With only minor modifications, Al Koran's 'The Pendulum Tells[24]' becomes a little gem that borders on the mystical, yet never leaves the realm of psychology. It is yet another variation on Pseudo Psychometry: you deliver brief readings for all the cards, then identify the authors with the help of a pendulum. This presentation makes sense only if you represent graphology accurately, without exaggerating its scope. It's also best not to perform any other experiment in which you identify the owner of a handwriting in the same show.

Aside from coded cards and identical pens, you'll need a pendulum. This can be anything from a ring or other small, reasonably hefty object tied to a piece of string, about 20–25 cm (8–10 in) long, even fashioned on the spot, to an expensive, 'professional' pendulum bought from a New Age store, dowsing supplier, or the like. A knot or small bead at the top of the string makes it easier to hold. Put the pendulum within easy reach, in your pocket or case.

Start as usual by handing out coded cards to all the participants, who write any word or brief sentence of your or their choosing on the back of their card while your back is turned, then have someone collect the cards, mix them and hand them to you as you face the audience again.

If you haven't already introduced the concept of graphology earlier in your act, do so now, explaining that handwriting reveals a lot about the writer. Caution the spectators not to let you know who wrote what, then proceed with the readings in the usual manner. Leave the discarded cards scattered on the table, writing side up.

---

24 In *Al Koran's Professional Presentations*.

"*Handwriting can tell us a lot about a person, but there's a lot it doesn't tell us.*" Gesture toward the cards: "*I can look at these and say, this was written by an optimist, this by a pessimist, etc., but I can't tell if it was written by a man or a woman—let alone identify the writer.*" Let this sink in for a moment, then continue, brightly: "*But I'm going to try anyway!*"

Deadpan: "*To do this, I'm going to need a high-precision scientific instrument.*" Bring out the pendulum so that it comes into view at the end of the sentence, holding it in normal 'dowsing' position: elbow resting on the table, forearm vertical or close to it, wrist bent forward but relaxed, the bead held between thumb and first finger, the tip of the pendulum about 2.5–5 cm (1–2 in) above the tabletop. "*A pendulum.*" Pause for a beat; you may get a chuckle or two from the line.

Put the pendulum on the table and address the audience: "*As you know, the subconscious makes connections that the conscious mind doesn't know exist. Sometimes they come out as hunches—what we call intuition. Having analysed thousands of handwritings, it's quite possible that I may be able to match the writing to the writer.*" While you deliver the above, gather the cards in your hands and turn the pile over so that the cards are writing side down. Casually mix the cards between the fingertips of both hands, ending with card number 4 on top; glance at the cards as needed to locate it. This is to build suspense and increase surprise later on. Put the pile on the table, slightly to the side.

Pick up the pendulum, put your arm in dowsing position again and look at the pendulum. *"The pendulum is simply a tool to communicate with the subconscious. If you ask a question and relax, the subconscious answers by making the pendulum move."*

Take the top card from the stack and put it on the table in front of you, writing side up. Adjust the position of your elbow so that the pendulum hangs above the centre of the card. Caution the spectators again not to give you any hint as to the identity of the writer. Ask spectator number one for her name, if you don't already know it; let's say it's Anne. Look at her for a moment, then focus on the card and say, as if to yourself: *"Did Anne write this?"* Remain silent and motionless for five or ten seconds, as if waiting for the pendulum to respond, then say: *"No."* Go through the same procedure with participants number two and three. For participant number four, the writer, slowly the pendulum begins to swing.

To do this, relax your hand as much as possible, hold the cord as loosely as you dare, and simply will the pendulum to move from side to side. The trick is to allow it to happen; if you relax enough, tiny, involuntary movements of your hand muscles will make the pendulum swing. You can just as easily will it to stop, to move back and forth or in a circle, to swing wildly or gently, and so on.

Allow the pendulum to swing noticeably for a few seconds, then pull your hand back to stop it. *"Yes! I believe that you wrote this"*, you say. Slide the card toward her and ask her to acknowledge this. Have her leave the card on the table in front of her, so you'll know to skip her for the remaining cards.

Repeat the procedure for the next card—nothing happens, the pendulum stays still. *"Hmm... was it beginner's luck, the first time?"* Appear deep in thought for a moment, then shrug and put the card on the bottom of the pile, saying that maybe you'll have better luck with another card.

Handle the next two cards the same way as the first one, reading the coded value as you remove each card from the stack. Remember always to stop the pendulum by moving your hand back, rather than by willing it to stop, to avoid anybody suspecting that you can control it consciously, and skip the writers you've already identified.

For clarity, let's say that the card you missed earlier belongs to John, and that the remaining spectator is Mary. John's card is below Mary's.

"*This leaves us with two cards—this one...*", slide Mary's card a few inches to the side, "*... and the one I didn't get earlier*", resting your fingertips on John's card. Appear deep in thought for a moment, then brightly: "*Let me try something.*" Slide the two cards toward yourself so that they're side by side and a few inches apart, in position for the pendulum. "*If I look at this card alone....*" Turn over John's card, look at it briefly and test it against both spectators. Nothing happens. Half to yourself: "*Then I still can't tell... but what if I look at the* other *card...?*" Turn over Mary's card, study it briefly, then put it down in the same position. Now test John's card against both spectators again—this time, the pendulum moves for John. Smiling: "*So, now my subconscious knows that this card has to be John's...*", pointing at his card, "*... because it knows that this one... is Mary's!*", pointing at hers. Continue, earnestly: "*But let me double-check....*" Check Mary's card against both spectators; the pendulum swings for Mary. Brightly: "*Yes!*"

Slide the two cards toward their respective owners, lean back and smile, then: "*It never ceases to amaze me what the subconscious mind can do!*" Take your bow.

SYMBOLISM

The 'Triple Prediction' effect lends itself well to a psychological presentation. The focus of the effect is on the spectator's intuition, rather than on the performer's ability to make predictions. This helps take much of the heat off the handling. It is also one of the few psychological effects in which near misses increase believability, just as in psychic presentations.

The most straightforward and elegant handling of the 'Triple Prediction' effect is, without doubt, Tony 'Doc' Shiels's 'Psychic CCC[25]', which is used here. You need three small slips of paper or business cards, a glass (optional) if using slips, a sheet of paper or a notepad, and a pen.

Pick a male volunteer and get his name—say, Alan. Ask Alan to pick a female volunteer and get her name—let's say, Betty. Hand Betty the sheet or notepad and the pen, and ask her to write something, for example, "*Hi, my name is Betty*". Take the pen and sheet back, appear to study the writing for a moment or two, then hand the sheet to Alan. "*I'm*

---

25 In his book, *Entertaining with ESP.*

going to make a note; in the meantime, have a good look at Betty's writing." Pick up the pen and a slip and write the word "*Rose*", holding the slip in front of you and the pen horizontal so that no one can see what you're writing. Put the pen down, fold the slip into quarters, writing side inward, and drop it into the glass or put it on the table. If using business cards, put the card on the table, writing side down.

"*Alan, you can put the sheet down now. Close your eyes and, without thinking, name... a type of landscape.*" If he hesitates, you can add: "*For example: a beach, a forest, a mountain... even a cityscape.*" When he answers, commit his choice to memory—let's say, meadow—and tell him that he can open his eyes.

Glance at the writing and note the slant. "*Betty, I have no idea if you like meadows, but I see from your handwriting that you're a very sociable person, so if you ever spend time in one, I'm sure it would be with lots of friends!*", smiling as you deliver the last part. If the slant is vertical or varying, you can describe the trait and ask her whether she'd want to be alone or with friends at this moment. Alternatively, you can simply mention any trait or two, as if you noticed it in passing.

Ask Betty to chose a male volunteer and get his name—let's say, Charles. "*Let me just make a note...*", pick up another slip and write down Alan's choice of landscape or something very similar; for example, instead of '*meadow*', you can write '*grassy field*'. Fold the slip and put it in the glass or on the table near the first one (if using a card, drop it on top of the first one).

Tell Betty to listen carefully as you ask Charles a few questions. The idea is to get him to talk; if appropriate, you can ask him if he remembers the Jack and Jill rhyme, for example, and have him recite a few lines. "*Betty, please close your eyes, and without thinking, name... a colour.*" Commit her answer to memory and tell her she can open her eyes

Ask Charles to select a female volunteer and get her name—let's say, Denise. State that you are making a note, write down Betty's choice of colour, and put the slip or card with the first two. Ask Charles a few questions about Denise, e.g.: what is the colour of her hair? Is it long or short? Is she wearing glasses? What colours is she wearing? Then: "*Charles, please close your eyes and, without thinking, name... a flower.*" After he answers, tell him he can open his eyes.

Address the audience: "*Whenever we become aware of something, we relate it to what we already know. Usually, it's to our own experience: this handwriting makes me think of so-and-so's, etc. But we can also relate things to more universal symbols. The shape and rhythm of a handwriting can remind us of a landscape; to describe sounds, we use words like colour and tone; a person's appearance can make us think of just about anything—even a flower.*" Pause briefly.

"*The goal of this experiment was to get you to access your intuition so that you could relate what you saw or heard to universal symbols. I wrote down the symbol most likely to be chosen for Betty's handwriting, Charles's voice, and Denise's appearance. Let's see how we did.*"

"*Alan, after looking at Betty's handwriting, you thought of...?*" At the same time, dump the slips onto the table and look through them to find the appropriate one, leaving the other ones folded. If using business cards, pick up all three, writing facing you. They will be in the order: flower, landscape, colour. Thumb the flower card into your other hand, fan the two remaining ones, look at all three cards, then put the flower and colour back on the table, writing side down, a few inches apart.

By this time, Alan will have named the landscape. "*And I wrote...*", read the slip, turn it toward Alan so he can read it and acknowledge. Do the same for the remaining slips and take your bow.

If Charles named a flower other than a rose, you can simply brush it off with something like: "*Two out of three—not bad!*" or you could pretend you're learning something new, you ask the rest of the audience to let you know which flower came to mind—the rose or Charles's choice— by a show of hands, and apparently make a mental note of the results.

A GRAPHOLOGICAL GAG

If you mix psychic and psychological presentations and you do any kind of spirit writing effect after you've already introduced the notion of graphology during the performance, here's a humorous tag line you can use. Reveal the writing and conclude the experiment as you normally would, then make some 'graphological' comment about the writing, such as: "*This spirit has a great love of life*", "*This spirit is very outgoing, a real people-person—er, people-spirit*", and so on.

Magic

MAGIC

Graphology isn't easily introduced into a magic performance. Practically the only time we ask a spectator to write something is when we need a card to be signed for later verification. For this purpose, the actual content of the writing is of no importance; it only matters that the card bear a unique mark. It might as well be a scribble—and that's often what we get. Rarely do we have a good sample of handwriting to analyse.

The obvious solution is to make the content of the writing relevant to the trick. This gives the spectator a reason to make an effort to write properly. Let's say that you do some version of the 'Floating Bill' trick. You have the spectator pick up a cocktail napkin and write on it the name of something that flies or floats, be it a hot air balloon, a species of bird or a favourite superhero. You take the napkin, tear off the quarter with the writing, do a brief analysis, perhaps relate the reading to what the spectator wrote, and proceed to make the napkin float. Heavy, non-textured napkins, such as cocktail napkins, are adequate for getting a reasonably good sample, especially if it's written with a pen, rather than a marker, which is likely to spread.

Another example is the trick, often seen in beginner's magic books, in which a business or playing card is inserted into an envelope, the envelope is cut in half, yet the card remains whole, thanks to a slit in the middle of the envelope. You could have the spectator write something on the card to act as a protective spell, such as 'Stainless steel' or 'Indestructible', or something more philosophical, like 'Love', to motivate the effect. Or even a very short incantation to make it into a quasi-Bizarre magic presentation.

This approach is particularly useful in card magic. For almost any trick, and particularly for tricks that involve motion in some fashion— the 'Card to Wallet', the 'Haunted Deck' or even the 'Ambitious Card'— you can have the spectator write the name of *"something that goes bump in the night"*: Gremlin, Poltergeist, Ghost or what have you. Or you could ask her to pick her favourite magic words: 'Abracadabra', 'Alakazam', a simple 'Poof!' or anything she likes—even 'Please', if she's so inclined or, if all else fails, simply 'Magic words'.

Story presentations open up other avenues. One example is the 'DYI Ambitious Card', from my book *Card Stories*. The presentation involves flowers, so it makes perfect sense to ask the spectator to write the name of her favourite flower on the card. (In a case like this, it also makes sense to learn a bit about the meaning of flowers in order to do a reading on the spectator's choice before analysing her handwriting.)

There are other ways in which the writing can be incorporated into a trick, or even become a central part of the effect itself. For example, it could influence the outcome: the spectator writes down the name of some object on a slip of paper, and you magically produce the actual object from the slip, as is (almost) the case in the trick 'Carl, the Character Cup', below. Or something could happen to the writing itself: the spectator writes something on a card, then the writing disappears and reappears, jumps from card to card, multiplies, changes into something else or maybe even changes colour, if that could be accomplished, and so on[26]. There are, no doubt, many more ideas waiting to be discovered and explored.

Lastly, why not perform one of the experiments described in the Mentalism section? It's certainly unusual for a magic act to incorporate those kinds of effects, but there's nothing particularly jarring about it, particularly when the effects are presented as psychological demonstrations. After all, we show our ability to read 'tells' in poker demonstrations, for example, so it's not a great stretch to demonstrate other psychological abilities.

Below are a few tricks built around the ideas described here. They can be used as is or as starting points for your own explorations.

GHOSTLY DEDUCTION

A volunteer selects a card, then writes a few words on a piece of paper. You get out your magnifying glass, study the writing, give a brief analysis and reveal the card, with a little help from the magnifier.

There's a dealer item that goes by various names, such as 'Ghost Glass'. It consists of a glass item (there are several models) that reveals the image of a playing card when you breathe on it. For this trick, the mag-

---

26 A good starting point is Paul Harris's 'Sliding Ink', in *Close-up Fantasies*, Book I, and also in *The Art of Astonishment*, Book 2.

nifying glass is ideal, but you can also use the spectacles or even the plain disk. You handle the disk as if it were a magnifier, or set it in a magnifying glass frame. Alternatively, you can make your own: magic dealers now sell a bottle of liquid that allows you to create the same effect on any glass object you like. Another way is to have the name of the card printed or engraved on the handle. In a pinch, or for simplicity, you can glue a tiny playing card in the middle of the glass. You'll just have to make sure that you don't expose the card prematurely.

To perform, force the appropriate card by your favourite method. Have the volunteer memorize it, show it to the rest of the audience, and replace it in the deck. Put the deck aside.

Hand the volunteer a slip of paper, a pen or marker, and a writing surface if necessary. You can have her write a few random words or a sentence, something appropriate to the venue, the occasion or your presentation, or something humorous. Take the slip from the spectator and explain that you're going to try to determine her card by studying her handwriting. Bring out the magnifying glass, study the writing and do a brief analysis. Pause briefly, then claim that you now know which card she selected and name it.

After this has sunk in, smile and say that it was actually the magnifying glass that told you which card she chose. Pause for half a beat, then say: "*No, really*", and reveal the image on the magnifier.

Alternatively, you can have the spectator write the name of any card in the deck, either the one she selected or a different one, and present the trick as a lie detector experiment. In this case, after you do the reading, study her handwriting again, then announce whether she wrote the truth or a lie. If it was a lie, study the slip some more and state that you can also detect which card she actually selected; pause briefly and name it. In either case, ask her if she knows how you knew and finish as above.

The spectacles and a few other Ghost Glass items allow you to reveal two cards. You can expand the trick by working with two spectators. These can be unrelated or a couple, in which case you can make some gentle, humorous statements regarding their compatibility or remarks about marriage or relationships in general.

If you like, you can present the trick with a Sherlock Holmes theme. This can be as simple or as elaborate as you like, from a mere mention of his name, to a big production, complete with deerstalker hat and calabash pipe. You could explain that you're going to deduce information from your observations; have the volunteer write the sentence: "The game's afoot!"; work in an "Elementary, my dear Watson", especially if you can coax the volunteer to say it; make some ridiculous claim during the analysis, such as: *"You are a retired sergeant of the Fifth Cavalry division"*, *"You own a stagecoach with two horses, one chestnut and one white"*, or what have you.

INK RISING

My friend Suzanne the Magician is a professional close-up worker from Minneapolis, Minnesota. In addition to her restaurant and corporate work, Suzanne performs regularly at the Magic Castle. She received the prestigious Close-Up Magician of the Year award for 2010 from the Academy of Magical Arts.

When I mentioned to Suzanne that I was working on a book on handwriting analysis, she immediately saw the possibilities this opened for incorporating incidental readings into a close-up performance. It is thanks to her vision that this chapter came into being.

In addition, Suzanne has graciously given me permission to describe a trick from her repertoire that's perfect for readings. It's a charming version of the 'Ambitious Card', done with blank cards and much humour[27]. The description below is transcribed from an actual performance at the Magic Castle, with a volunteer named Vince.

To prepare, get a deck of blank-both-sides cards and put three cards aside. Put the deck in a regular card case and put it in your right jacket pocket, together with a marker. Take a regular deck of cards and cut an Ace (not Spades) to the bottom. Cover the Ace with a blank card and put the two remaining blanks on the top of the deck. Put the deck in your left jacket pocket, the top of the deck nearest your body.

To perform, take the case from your right pocket and hand it to your volunteer. Address the volunteer: *"Please shuffle the deck. The reason I have you shuffle the cards is because a lot of people think that I put them in a certain order, and I don't want anybody to think I do that. Well, that*

---

27 Suzanne was inspired by 'Seth Kramer's Blank Ambition', published in Steven Schneiderman's *Ruminations*, volume 1, issue 5.

would be cheating, and we just met. I would not cheat you... well, not right away, anyway... maybe in a minute." When he's done shuffling, take the deck back.

"*I'm going to fan these out toward you. Please pick any card you want. ... Don't let me see it. ... Ok, show it around. ... Do you like that one, or would you like to trade? ... I'm going to dribble the cards like this and you say 'stop'. ... Put your card right there. You won't forget it, will you?*" Fan the cards so that the audience can see the 'faces', then turn to the spectator and have him pick a card as you look away. After going through the standard bits of business, dribble the cards until the spectator stops you, have the card replaced on the lower half, turn the hand holding the upper half palm up and stare at the face card, as if you're memorizing a key card. Pause for the reaction, then slap the upper half onto the bottom portion and square.

"*Now I'm going to find your card. I just snap my fingers and... no, that's not it. I'll just snap my fingers again—this one? ... No? You know, I bet you can do it. Here, just snap your fingers... there. How did you do? Turn over the top card... and there it is! Everybody, give him a big hand! ... You are amazing.*" Snap your fingers, show the 'face' of the top card, bury the card in the middle and repeat. Then have the spectator do the same and claim that he found his card again. Have him show it around as the audience applauds. End with the card on the table in front of the spectator.

"*I have no idea how you could tell that that was your card, since these are all blank. You know what would make it easier for me? It would be easier if your card looked different from these, so if you could write your name on the face... oops, sorry—on the face of the card.*" Hand the marker to the spectator and pretend that the card is face down, so you turn it face up. Have him sign it, then take the marker back and put it in your right outer jacket pocket.

"*So—how can you tell that this is your card?*" Acknowledge the answer; at the same time, get a break under the top card of the deck. Take the spectator's card, place it on top, writing side up, and square. Rub the card, implicitly showing that the ink doesn't come off.

Now you do a very brief reading on one or two signs, pointing them out and explaining their significance. Suzanne suggests pretending to notice something as you look at the writing, for example: "*Oh, this is interesting. Are you...? See, your writing has... and that means....*" Alternatively, you can introduce the reading more formally, for example by explaining that a signature not only identifies the writer, but also reveals something about his or her personality.

"You see, this is what I was trying to do earlier. I took your card and put it in the middle of the deck, like this. Then, when I snapped my fingers, I thought that it had popped to the top of the deck. But I couldn't tell, because earlier, the card didn't say Vince on it." Turn over the two cards above the break as one, then insert the top card into the middle of the deck. Snap your fingers, look at the spectator as you continue talking and turn over the top card as you say the last few words. Show the card to the audience and get a break under the top card of the deck. Let the reaction die down, then put the card, writing side up, on the deck.

"This is what we were trying to do before. Remember, I put your card in the deck, like this. Now snap your fingers... perfect. How did you do?" Turn the double card over and insert the top card into the middle of the deck. After the spectator snaps his fingers, push the top card to the right so that he can turn it over. Have him show the card around and get the audience to applaud.

"I'm going to tell you how it works. Just don't tell anybody that I told you, though. ... It's the pen. That's how it works—it's the pen. ... Well, it didn't work until we brought the pen out, did it?" Here, you switch decks as you search for the pen and bring it out[28]. The switch is based on a sequence of actions done with a 'right-left, right-left, right-left' rhythm, rather than on sleight-of-hand, as follows.

Pat your right outer jacket pocket, then your left. Put your right hand in the pocket and rummage for a moment, as if searching for something, eventually grasping the marker. As soon as the right hand is in the pocket, put your left in the left pocket and exchange decks. Now bring your right hand, with the marker, out of your pocket, then your left, which is now holding the regular deck with the extra blanks.

Drop the pen on the table, point to it and continue talking.

"The magic is in the pen. That's why they call it a magic marker. ... I'm serious! You don't believe me? ... Watch your name—see, I can wipe it right off the card... and put it on my jacket." Pick up the card and put it on the deck, writing side up. Continue talking, then do an Erdnase col-

---

28 This is Tommy Wonder's pocket switch, described in *The Books of Wonder*.

our change or any change that leaves the signed card face up and second from the top. Continuing from the colour change, pretend to slap the ink onto your jacket (or other dark article of clothing or object nearby). If there's nothing dark enough within reach, simply toss it in the air with an appropriate line.

"You can't see it, because the ink is black and so is my jacket. … Let me try to put it back. See, it's not on the card. Now, where did I put it?" Do a double turnover to show that the card is blank on both sides, then take the top card by its inner corner and rub it wherever you slapped the ink previously. As you do this, get a break under the top card of the deck.

Show that the name is back on the card, then put the card on the deck, writing side up. Let the reaction subside.

"You may think that there's something funny about the card, so I'm going to put it aside, where I can't do anything without you seeing it." Do a double turnover and place the top card on the table, to the side and out of reach of the audience.

"Now I'm going to take another card and write my name on it." Deal the top card to the table in front of you, pick up the pen and write your name on it. The spectator's name is on the underside.

"So here we have a Suzanne card… and here, a Vince card." Pick up the card near you between your right thumb on top and fingers below, near the middle of the right long edge. Hold the other card in place by touching it with your left fingertips as you scoop it up with the card in your right. Continue the motion by pushing the lower card to the left and pulling the upper one to the right as you rotate your hand palm down. Take both cards in your left hand, rotate your right palm up again, then take one card in each hand.

"You remember I said that it's not the card, but the special ink. Did I tell you how the ink works? … It works by magic! … Yes, from the magic marker. Watch what happens when I flick it, like this … There! Did you see it?" Brush one card across the face of the other several times, quickly and noisily. The last time, exchange the cards and show that the ink has 'jumped' from one card to the other. This should get a chuckle. When it's over, slowly turn over the blank card and drop it on the table. After a short pause for the reaction, slowly turn the other card over to show that it now has both signatures on it. Acknowledge the reaction, then hand the card to the spectator.

"You can keep that. It'll be worth something some day. See, it says 'Vince' on it." Pause, then: *"Do you want to help me with something else? I'd like to do more magic with these cards, Vince. It's hard to do magic with these cards, though. Do you know why? … Yes! Because they're blank. That's exactly it! In fact, they're blank on both sides. But if I wanted to, I could fix them. In fact, if I wanted, I could fix all of them. Even on that side, too."* Pick up the deck, slide out the bottom card, show both sides as you talk about the cards being blank and drop the single card on the table. Take the deck in dealing position, rotate your hand palm down and thumb off the top card to the table. Since the face card is an ace, the protruding corners will be blank, which helps maintain the illusion of a blank deck. Say that you can fix the deck, snap your fingers and turn your hand palm up to reveal a printed back. After it sinks in, spread the cards to show that they all have backs, then show the faces on the other side. Segue into your favourite ambitious card routine.

You can use any suitable colour change you like instead of the sequence above. If you use one in which you steal a card from the bottom, then prepare the deck by placing one blank card on top and two on the face, rather than the other way around.

IMAGINARY CREATURES

A cute little trick with a cute little story. You show three blank-faced cards and have the spectator write the name of an imaginary creature on one—say, 'Unicorn'. As you tell the story of how you, as a child, saw unicorns everywhere, you show that all three cards say 'Unicorn', then they're all blank, then they all say 'Unicorn' again, and to end, they all say 'IMAGINATION'.

The method described below is based on Edward Victor's 'E-Y-E' trick, but you can just as easily use Marlo's 'Quick Three-Way' or any of its many variations, Boris Wild's 'Kiss' count, Jean Pierre Vallarino's 'Rumba' count, Brother Hamman's 'Flushtration' count, or any other method that allows you to show three cards as being identical.

Hold three playing cards in dealing position in left hand, face down. Press the ball of your thumb on the outer left corner of the packet and push to the right; with enough downward pressure, the flesh engages the top two cards and moves them to the right, perfectly aligned, while the bottom card remains in place by friction. Flip the double card over sideways to show the face of the (second) card and square the cards with your left hand only. Repeat to turn the (double) card face down, then transfer the top, single card to the bottom of the packet; square with your left hand only. The second time, you appear to do exactly the same thing, but here you turn over the top, single card, and transfer a double card to the bottom. The third time is the same as the first: you turn over a double card and transfer a single card to the bottom.

To prepare, get three blank-faced cards with regular, matching backs. With a permanent marker, write the word 'IMAGINATION' across the face of one card in very large letters. Hand-drawn lettering is preferable to a typographic look, which would jar with the spectator's handwritten word. To set up, put the 'imagination' card on top of the two others, all face down. Put the packet in your left jacket pocket, faces outward. Have a medium-tip permanent marker within easy reach.

"*I'd like to tell you an imaginary story with imaginary cards. Or, more accurately, an imaginary story with semi-imaginary cards. You see, they're normal on one side—and imaginary on the other.*" Take the packet from your pocket in dealing position, face down, and do the basic sequence described above to show three blank-faced cards. When done, put the packet on the table, near you.

"*The story involves an imaginary creature. I would like you to pick one. It can be anything you like: a dragon, a Heffalump, an honest politician... no, that's just too far-fetched.*"[29] After the reaction dies down, address the spectator again: "*Have you decided on an imaginary creature?*" Let's say the spectator names a unicorn. "*Ok. Now please write the word 'Unicorn' here, in your normal handwriting.*" Turn over the top card of the tabled packet, place it in front of the spectator, and hand her the marker. When she's finished writing, take the marker and the card. If the writing is small or very light, you can give it more presence by drawing a border around the edge of the card. Put the marker away and study the writing for a moment. "*I'm just looking at your handwriting.*" Point to a sign or two and do a brief reading. While still looking at the card, pause for a beat, then add: "*There's one more thing I can tell from what you wrote....*" Look her in the eye and say, very seriously: "*You like unicorns.*"

---

29 Thanks go to Steve Sharp for his 'honest politician' line.

While the audience reacts, continue looking at the spectator, turn the card face down and use it to scoop up the two cards on the table into your left hand. Quickly square the packet with your left hand only, and continue by apparently putting the bottom card on top. In fact, hold the top card between your right thumb at the back and fingers in front, and with the help of your left fingers, take the bottom two cards as one and put the double card on top. Square.

"*So, let me tell you the story. Once, when I was a little boy, my mom took me for a walk. I said: 'Oh, look, ma—there's a unicorn over here... and there's a unicorn over there... there are unicorns everywhere!'*" Do the basic sequence to show three 'unicorn' cards.

"*Mom said to me: 'Oh no, honey. There's no unicorn over here... and there's no unicorn over there... in fact, there are no unicorns anywhere! Unicorns don't exist.'*" Do the basic sequence to show three blank cards, but at the end, transfer a double card from top to bottom instead of a single.

"*I said: 'Oh, no, mom—you're wrong. There is a unicorn over here... and there is a unicorn over there... and there are unicorns everywhere. But remember: this is an imaginary story, so you have to imagine the unicorn over here... and imagine the unicorn over there... and imagine unicorns everywhere!'*" Do the basic sequence to show three unicorns and transfer a double card from top to bottom again. Pause while you say "*But remember: this is an imaginary story*", then do the basic sequence again to show the imagination card. Put the cards away and say, "*And that's my imaginary story.*"

For a different presentation, you choose a man and a woman—a couple, if possible—and have each one write the name of their favourite television show on a blank card. Let's say that John chooses a sports show and Mary, a cooking show. You do the trick exactly as above, with John wanting to watch his show on Saturdays, and on Sundays, and on every day of the week, then you do the same for Mary. You either skip the third phase or use it to illustrate that Mary was getting sick of sports shows. You pause to explain that they discussed the problem, then show that they solved it by giving up television altogether, with a card that says 'NO TV', the 'O' being a red, barred circle over a stylized television set, or that they took up a new pastime, such as Scrabble®, spelled out on tiles, or bridge, spelled out on a fan of playing cards, or anything that strikes your fancy, from tiddlywinks to tiger hunting.

With a bit of imagination, the concept can be applied to other packet tricks. For example, Dai Vernon's 'Twisting the Aces' can be used—with the names of three pet dogs and one cat, written on blank-faced cards—to demonstrate that dogs can be trained to obey commands, but cats cannot. You handle the cat card exactly as you would the Ace of Spades in the original version, explaining that cats do as they please for the final reversal.

For this effect, it makes more sense to do the readings after the trick. You thank the spectators for "*lending you their pets for the experiment*" by doing a brief handwriting analysis for each one. Alternatively, you say, tongue in cheek, that "*pets often take on the character of their owner*", and proceed to "*analyse the pets's handwriting*".

Another example is Peter Kane's 'Wild Card', which you can use to turn eight cards with drawings of weeds into drawings of flowers, after the spectator writes 'I love flowers' on the single blank-faced card in the middle. Although it's unusual for the 'wild' card to be different from both the 'before' and 'after' cards, there's no technical reason to prevent this. You may have to adjust the handling slightly, though, so that the written card is involved in every one of the eight transformations.

TRADING PLACES

A comedy bit in which you and a spectator magically trade places, or so you claim, ending with a signature transposition using business cards.

Set up by placing a small packet of business cards, all similarly oriented and facing the same way, in your left jacket pocket, blank sides toward your body. Have a pen or a marker with a thin tip handy.

"*Signatures are fascinating things. They reflect who we are, they capture a bit of our essence, our uniqueness.... For what follows, I would like to borrow someone's signature for a few minutes. May I borrow yours? I promise to give it back at the end.*"

Choose an attractive woman (or a fit-looking man, if you're a woman), who has obviously been enjoying your performance, reacts easily and doesn't seem shy.

Reach into your pocket to remove the packet of business cards. As soon as you've grasped it, thumb off the face card and leave it behind as you take your hand out of your pocket. Put the packet on the table in front of the spectator, hand her the pen and ask her to write her normal signature on it, as if she were writing a cheque. When she's finished writing, take the packet.

"Thank you. Now I can cash my business card... Oh, I'm sorry! I was going to tell you how our signature reflects who we are. Let's see..." Study the signature for a moment, then do a brief reading on one or two traits, pointing out and explaining the signs. Let this sink in.

"To a magician, a signature is more than just a reflection of a person— it's the person's very essence. Abracadabra ... I am now you!" Hold the packet in your left hand, writing side up. Put your right hand over your left and close your eyes for a moment, then open your eyes, look at the spectator and deliver the last few words.

"Do you like my hair? ... I love this dress! It makes me feel like royalty ... and it goes so well with this nail polish... These shoes are gorgeous, but the heels are killing me...." Make as much fun of the situation, of a man wearing women's clothing, as you like. Address both the spectator and the rest of the audience, getting everybody to join in the game and 'admire' you.

"Now, if I'm you, then it's only fair for you to become... me! Don't worry, it won't hurt a bit. Let me hold onto your signature for a moment... while I give you mine." Push her card a bit to the right with your left thumb and hold your hand up for everyone to see, as you say that you'll hold onto her signature, then put your hand in your pocket, apparently to thumb the card off and leave it there. In fact, you pull the card back, cover it with the blank card that you left behind at the beginning, and square the packet as you bring your hand out. The whole process should take but a moment, since you're apparently just dropping the card into your pocket.

As you talk about giving her your signature, take the pen and sign the face card, keeping the packet in your hand, rather than on the table. This will help motivate your actions later on. Put the pen away.

"Let's see what my signature says about me... highly intelligent, impeccable character, a born leader of men, possessor of great mystical powers... actually, I'm making that up." Deliver the 'analysis' mock seriously, then face the audience and grin for the last part. You can point to the same signs that you analysed in the spectator's signature earlier, and explain their meaning in yours, or you can simply move on. In any case, show your signature to the audience.

"Now you only have to hold my signature between your palms. Would you hold out your hand, please?... put your other hand on top... perfect!"

As the audience sees it, you push the face card forward a bit, turn your hand palm down and place the outjogged card on the spectator's hand. In fact, you're going to push a double card forward and do a variation of the glide, which will leave her with her signature instead of yours. You could use the standard glide here, but this variation is much more deceptive and also gives you a second chance to separate the bottom card from the one above. This is often necessary with business cards because they tend to cling together, especially if they're printed on rough-textured stock.

Tilt your left hand forward a bit by rotating your wrist outward. This will help conceal the extra thickness of the double card. Place the tips of your right first and second fingers on the face of the card, and the very corner of your thumbnail at the near edge of the packet. Apparently push the card forward with the first two fingers, but in fact, your thumbnail engages two cards and pushes them forward, perfectly aligned, about 1 cm (½ in). If you find it difficult to engage exactly two cards, you can get a small break below the two face cards as you toy with the packet after you put the pen away.

Make sure that your left little finger contacts the near edge of the packet, as for any version of the glide. Now rotate both hands simultaneously at the wrists, the left inward and the right outward, your right fingers remaining in contact with the face card. During the rotation, move your hands just a bit closer together, or extend your two right fingers a bit more; this effectively pushes the face card to the left, until it butts against the left little finger. If the two cards didn't fully separate, push the bottom one to the left in a rubbing motion between your right thumb and fingers; this helps keep the upper card from moving. In either case, be very careful not to flash the outer corner of the bottom card when pushing it to the left. It's also a good idea to tilt the front of the packet downward a bit to help conceal the motion.

Without changing the position of your hands, bend your right first finger so that its tip is opposite your thumb, grasp the single projecting card and move your hands in opposite directions. Continue by putting the card on the spectator's outstretched hand and have her put her other hand on top. You may want to touch the back of her hand lightly with your fingertips as you tell her to keep her hands together. If you're very concerned about the spectator opening her hands and exposing her signature prematurely, put the card on the table and have her put both hands on it. Openly, but without calling attention to it, put the packet in your pocket.

"*Abracadabra—and now... you are me! ... You look so dapper in that suit! Look at those broad shoulders... those bulging muscles... that full head of hair... What a man!*" Now you can make fun of yourself, for as long as it amuses the audience.

"*Tonight, I can go home and relax in a nice bubble bath... and tomorrow, you can go to my great-great-great-aunt's funeral... that's after my dentist appointment.... What's that?... You'd rather not? Oh... it's just as well, I guess—I look ridiculous in this dress, don't I... besides, I hate bubble baths.*" You talk about any suitable pleasant and unpleasant situations matter-of-factly, without appearing deceitful, then you pretend to overhear the spectator being unhappy at the prospect of taking your place and act surprised at first, then understanding.

"*So—let me put things back the way they were.... Abracadabra! Now I'm me again... and you're you. See for yourself.*" Rummage a bit through your pocket, as if looking for something, and grasp the packet of business cards. As you bring your hand out, push the face card halfway off the packet and at an angle, so that it looks like the card she signed was separated from the packet. Take the card in your right hand, glance at it briefly, as if making sure you've got the right card, then hold the card face down as you put the packet back in your pocket or on the table. As you say the magic word, slowly and drawn out, flutter your left fingers a few inches above the card and continue as you extend your arm toward the spectator's hands, then back again to your card. Turn the card over to show that it now has your signature on it as you claim to be yourself again, then gesture toward the spectator when you deliver the last part. Drop your card on the table as she looks at the card she's holding. Have her show it around and take your bow.

If you prefer, you can do the trick with first names instead of signatures. They're just as personal, and they allow you to add a light mystical or spiritual touch to the effect, if you so desire.

GOOD ADVICE

A personality test that magically proves the accuracy of its results, with a little help from the 'Out to Lunch' principle[30].

The cards should be big enough for the spectator to write on comfortably, without feeling cramped for space. Index cards, either 7.5 x 12.5 cm (3 x 5 in) or 10 x 15 cm (4 x 6 in) work well.

You can have the cards professionally printed, or you can print them yourself on the back of custom-printed promotional postcards, on store-bought blank index cards (either 3 x 5 or 4 x 6 in), or on letter-sized sheets of card stock that you cut into quarters. If using the latter, make sure that all the cards are exactly the same width, to avoid exposing the method. Use any images you like, or scan the ones provided below and size them appropriately.

---

30 Although the 'Out to Lunch' principle is associated with Edward Bagshawe, it doesn't seem that he ever claimed credit for it. Its use goes back to mediumistic stunts of the 19th century.

You'll need one 'before' card for every 10 to 20 'after' cards. Print as many cards as you like, cut the 'before' cards in half and discard the bottom, blank portion. To make a packet, stack 10 to 20 'after' cards, all facing the same way, put a 'before' half-card on top so that it covers the image on the card below it, square the packet carefully so that the half-card is perfectly aligned with the top edge and sides of the whole cards and wrap a wide rubber band around the middle of the packet, concealing the edge of the half-card. The rubber band should hold the cards together tightly, but not so tightly that they buckle. If necessary, wrap the band around more than once, but in such a way that it doesn't prevent the packet from lying reasonably flat on the table.

If, after performing the trick for a while, you decide that you like it and print up a sizeable batch of cards, set them up in ready-to-go packets and store them in plastic bags or in boxes to prevent them from discolouring and getting dusty, but keep the rubber bands separate. They decompose with age, heat and sunlight and risk ruining the cards.

To perform, have the packet and a pen or thin-tipped marker at hand. Address the audience. *"Do you ever do those pop quizzes you find in magazines? ... I do them all the time. Just the other day, I found out that I'd make a terrific girlfriend and that I should wear blue eyeshadow."* Pause briefly for any reaction you get from the last line.

"Some time ago, a friend wondered whether she'd make a good advice columnist. I couldn't find a test for that in my magazine collection, so I came up with one for her. Here, why don't you try it..." If possible, choose a female spectator who seems good-natured and has been enjoying your performance. Such a spectator is most likely to be willing to play along.

Bring out the packet and show the drawing around: *"As you see, Sally the sparrow is displeased with her beau, for whatever reason. What do you think he should do to get back in her good graces?"* Address the participant as you ask the question and wait for her answer.

"'Give her flowers and chocolate'? Ok—write your piece of advice here, please: 'Give Sally flowers and chocolate'." Acknowledge her answer and repeat it. Point to the bottom half of the card as you tell her to write her answer there, starting with *"Give Sally..."*. This way, you have at least one descender to help you determine the dominant zone later on, as long as she doesn't write in block letters.

Hand her the pen and put the packet on the table in front of her so that she can write comfortably. If you like, hold the upper corners, away from the writing area, as if holding the packet in place for her, but actually making sure that the half card remains aligned with the packet. When she's finished writing, put the pen away and pick up the packet.

"Flowers are the typical romantic gift. If you really love flowers, you're probably sentimental and enjoy poetry. Chocolate is a romantic gift too. It means that you're sensuous: you enjoy physical sensations—food, textures, working with your hands, and so on." You interpret her answer in a very straightforward way. For example:

Flowers, music, card, love letter, poem: sentimental, poetic
Apology: sensitive, emotional
Chocolate, wine, candy, perfume, bird seed: sensuous
Wedding ring, jewellery, clothes, worms, nest: practical, down to earth
Book, museum: thinker, intellectual
Comedy, amusement park: fun-loving
Movie, play: interpret according to the genre

and so on. You should have no problem finding a simple interpretation for any choice. Be sure to point out the romantic aspect of the answer.

Do a reading on her dominant zone (pick one if there are several), then tie it to her answer, if possible, and highlight the aspect that fits with giving advice. For example: *"These big lower loops in your handwriting mean that you're motivated by your instincts, your body and the material world. You probably enjoy physical activity, the way things feel and taste, and making money. You may be involved in business, sports, food, real estate, or something manual, like chiropractic or pottery."* Pause briefly, then: *"Flowers and chocolate reflect your preference for the physical world and the experiences of the senses—the smell of flowers, the taste of chocolate."* Pause briefly again, then continue: *"Your advice is based not only on your sense of romance, but also on your instincts, which are well developed. I think you'd make an excellent advice columnist!"* For the middle zone, highlight feelings; for the upper zone, highlight understanding.

Hold the packet in your left hand so that the writing faces you and the illustration is nearest the floor. With your right fingertips, separate the face card from the rest, then grip the card between thumb and first finger as you turn your left hand palm down and pull the card out with your right. This effectively hides the face of the card. Place it on the table near you and put the packet away, out of sight in your pocket or case. You can handle the packet freely because it still shows the 'before' illustration, which is as it should be, but you want the packet to be out of sight at the end of the trick to avoid anybody focusing on the rubber band.

"Now let's see if the others agree. Put your fingertips on the edge of the card… and everybody join in. I'd like you all to imagine that you're Sally, receiving flowers and chocolate. … You can all let go of the card now. So what do you think—will it work? Will Sally soon be back with her beau?" Put your fingers on the nearest edge of the card as you tell her to do the same. If the spectator's answer is typically romantic, have everybody near her join in, otherwise let her do it alone. You want the audience to agree that the spectator's answer is likely to get Sally and her beau back together again, but not everybody would agree that taking Sally bungee jumping, if that's what she suggests, is the best way to accomplish this.

Give the audience some time to process your request, and wait until no more answers are forthcoming. Hold onto the card throughout.

"*Yes, I think so too. Turn over the card, please.*" Push the card toward the spectator and withdraw your hand. Make sure that everybody sees the change, then wait for the reaction to die down.

"*So if you ever decide to quit your job, you can have a new career as an advice columnist. ... Now tell me honestly: do you think that I'd look good with blue eyeshadow?*" Ask the question in a serious, even somewhat worried, tone, and with appropriate expressions.

CARL, THE CHARACTER CUP

A colour reading, a graphology reading, and a fun magical production. The spectator picks one of several pens from a cup and writes her name. You explain what her choice of ink colour means and how it relates to a particular sign in her handwriting. With much byplay, you end by producing from the cup a rubber ball of the same colour as the pen she used.

You will need from three to eight pens or markers of different colours, matching rubber balls, a cup or small, opaque tumbler, and a notepad, index cards or loose slips for the spectator to write on. The pens should have caps the same colour as the ink, rather than, say, small dots to indicate colour, so that it's immediately obvious to the volunteer that they're all different. The cup can be from a cups and balls set or anything else that can hold the pens comfortably without tipping over or the pens falling out. The balls should be big enough so that, once you load one into the mouth-down cup, you don't have to reach deep inside with your little finger to hold it in place.

Everything goes in your close-up case. You must be able to locate the ball of the correct colour at a glance or by touch, and steal it without fumbling as you put the pens back into the case.

"*I would like someone who is having a good time to assist me.*" Select a well-behaved spectator who is obviously enjoying the performance and invite her to sit on your right. Greet her and get her name; let's say, Mary. Hand her the cup and the pens, asking her to put the pens in the cup. Pretend to take a few moments to find the notepad. Put it in front of her.

"*I would like you to write something about yourself. Since you seem to be having a good time, you can write: 'Mary is happy', in your normal handwriting.*" This gives you a few extra descenders, which you may need for the analysis. If you like, you can use the old gag: "*Are you having a good time? Say 'yes'"*, without pausing between sentences. When she's finished writing, have her replace the pen in the cup. Take the notepad.

"Our choices are not random. Whether we are aware of it or not, what we choose reflects who we are. You picked..." Glance at the notepad, then name the colour she chose and explain its symbolism. Adjust the explanation, if necessary, so that it can be related to a graphological sign. For example, red, which symbolizes vitality, energy, action, can be related to pressure. Green, which symbolizes nature and earth, can be related to the lower zone. Blue, which represents calmness and tranquility, can be related to the baseline. Detailed interpretations are given in 'Pentachrome', in the Mentalism section. Pause for a moment.

"Our handwriting isn't random, either. Every motion we make also reflects who we are. This is very apparent in our handwriting, which is a record of our motions." Point out the appropriate sign and explain its meaning very briefly. Pause for a moment, then interpret the sign as it relates to the colour reading. If the sign is strong, explain that it reinforces the choice of colour. If it's weak, explain that she may desire what the colour represents. Let's say the spectator chose red. If her writing shows good pressure, you explain that both red and strong pressure mean that she has the energy to get things done; if the pressure is weak, you explain that light pressure shows that she may feel the need for more energy to accomplish her goals.

After this has sunk in, tear off the sheet with her writing, put it on the table and replace the notepad in your case. Take the pens with your right hand and transfer them to your left. Replace them in the case and take the ball of the appropriate colour in position for loading into the cup. Take the cup with your right hand, turn it over and place it squarely on the ball in your left hand, which has come out of the case in the mean time. The hands meet just behind the edge of the table. After the cup is transferred, move your right hand out of the way and the left up to chest level, holding the cup between your left thumb and fingers, the tip of the little finger keeping the ball in place. All of this takes only a moment; you cover it by addressing the spectator: *"And now, let's get independent verification!"* It's a good idea to tilt the cup ever so slightly forward and to the right, so that the rim helps to hide the little finger, which is holding the ball in place, from the volunteer and the rest of the audience.

"Mary, meet my helper: this is Carl, the Character Cup!" Draw a pair of cartoon eyes on the cup with a marker or grease pencil, and bring it to life, like you would a puppet in a kid show. Give it a name, have it interact with the spectator, whisper in your ear and reply to it, and so on. End by producing the ball into the spectator's cupped, waiting hands: make a tossing motion with the cup and bend your little finger out of the way, projecting the ball into the spectator's hands, or bring the cup down quickly but gently onto her hands, bending the little finger as you get near. *"Carl agrees that red is, indeed, your colour!"*, naming the actual colour of the ball.

At the time of this writing, the popular Harry Potter novels are still in people's minds, so you can introduce the cup with something like: *"Perhaps you've heard of the Sorting Hat? Well, this is the Character Cup!"*

A little extra...

A LITTLE EXTRA...

Although the information provided in the Graphology section is all you need to do graphology readings, even as a full-time reader, you may like the idea of expanding your knowledge a bit. Here you will find some 'bonus' material that allows you to extend your offerings beyond the basics already described. Below are some additional graphological signs, followed by an intriguing way of applying your knowledge of graphology to something other than handwriting.

SPECIFIC FORMATIONS

Most of the signs previously discussed apply to the whole of a handwriting. Here we look at a few signs related to specific shapes of strokes and letters. In a full reading, these signs are significant only if they occur with a certain regularity, otherwise they should be considered accidental and thus discarded. In a short or incidental reading, however, they're worth mentioning anyway, because they give the impression of great insight and may highlight a trait that is so typical of the writer that it creates great amusement among her friends.

When these signs are present in a handwriting, they indicate the presence of the corresponding trait; however, their absence does not mean that the trait is absent. Also, many signs do not have a symbolic interpretation; their meaning should simply be memorized.

There's no need to modify the tick sheet to include these traits. It's more practical simply to write them in the Comments section. You should have no trouble composing appropriately neutral or positive lines for all the traits below.

Loops

Loops in the three zones are grouped together here only for ease of memorization. They are not otherwise related to each other.

In the upper zone
The loops formed by the ascenders of the lower-case letters 'b', 'h', 'k', and 'l' represent our perspective, how we look at new situations. Sym-

183

bolically, the **size of the loops** indicate the capacity for **imagination**. Full, rounded loops mean that the writer is *imaginative*, capable of seeing many possibilities. Narrow loops indicate a *practical* view. Stick-like ascenders, formed by a vertical downstroke only, without an initial upstroke, mean that the writer *sees only the facts*.

These interpretations apply only to cleanly shaped loops that are proportional to the handwriting, not to loops that are irregular, disproportionate or otherwise distorted.

In the middle zone
If the downstrokes inside the lower case letters 'm' and 'n' are in the shape of loops, the writer is prone to *worrying*.

In the lower zone
If the descenders of the lower-case 'j', 'p' and 'y' end abruptly at the bottom, the writer tends to be *abrupt*. If they're looped, the writer is likely to have a *friendly* manner.

brown　　　*brown*　　　*brown*

many　　　*many*　　　*many*

T-bars

The lower-case 't' reveals a mass of information about how we relate to our work, to the tasks we perform. For our purposes, only a few formations of the cross-bar are of interest.

The **pressure** of the cross-bar, relative to the pressure of the whole handwriting, indicates **will** and **willpower**. A strong cross-bar means that the writer is most likely to see projects through in spite of difficulties, whereas a weak cross-bar means that the writer is more likely to give up when faced with too many obstacles.

The **vertical placement** of the cross-bar relative to the stem indicates the writer's goal orientation. A low cross-bar means that the writer *underestimates* her ability, and therefore sets low goals for herself. A cross-bar at average height indicates *practical* goals. A cross-bar placed high on the stem means that the writer has *distant* goals, and a cross-bar above the stem indicates lofty, *visionary* goals.

The **horizontal placement** of the bar indicates the writer's **approach** to tasks. A bar that's longer on the left of the stem than on the right indicates *hesitation* or *indecision*. A balanced bar, more or less equal on both sides, indicates *reflection, caution*. A bar longer on the right than on the left indicates *initiative*.

Sometimes, the bar barely touches the stem, if at all. When it's entirely to the left, the writer tends to *procrastinate*. Entirely to the right, the writer is *impatient*.

A knotted cross-bar indicates *patience* and *persistence*, and a wavy cross-bar indicates a *sense of humour*.

Initial and final strokes

When the initial stroke, the stroke that starts the first letter of a word, is wavy, it means that the writer has a *sense of humour* (same as a wavy cross-bar). An initial stroke that starts with a small, reversed loop indicates *competitiveness*.

When the final stroke, the stroke at the very end of a word, curves upward and outward (to the right), it indicates *generosity*. This is true even if the stroke continues by looping back to the left.

Closed letters

The loops of the lower-case 'a' and 'o' reflect our **openness**. When these loops are open at the top, the writer is very *communicative*, perhaps even talkative. Clear, rounded loops, formed without extra loops or other marks, indicate *frankness*. Loops with an extra loop on the right mean that the writer is *secretive*.

boats   *boats*   *boats*

Specific shapes

o Words that taper, the letters getting progressively smaller, are a sign of *diplomacy*.

o An *ability with words*, from being a writer to enjoying Scrabble™ or crossword puzzles, can be seen in the following signs:

- lower-case 'f', 'g', 's', or upper-case 'S' in the shape of a figure '8'
- upper- or lower-case 'e' in the shape of an Epsilon or Celtic 'e'
- lower-case 'd' in the shape of a Delta.

fox   *dog*   *Sweets*

Ease   *Ease*   *dared*

Exercise 4

Go through the samples from the previous exercises, including the samples you collected yourself, and look for these additional signs.

Going further

If you want to learn more about graphology, there are plenty of excellent books available. I particularly recommend the works of Klara Roman (may be hard to find, but worth it), Andrea McNichol and Reed Hayes.

THE TREE TEST

Psychologists have a huge variety of tests at their disposal to evaluate all kinds of things. One of these is the 'Tree Test', in which subjects as young as three years old are asked to draw a tree. The drawing is used to help determine the subject's personality and uncover personality problems and disorders.

Most of the knowledge required to interpret the drawings comes from research done on the 'Tree Test' itself and a few similar tests, but some of it comes from different sources. What interests us here is something called the 'theory of the symbolism of space', devised by the Swiss graphologist Max Pulver. This theory is none other than the material covered in the Graphology section at the beginning of this book. As long as you know your zones, slants, margins and so on, you can do a basic reading of drawings of trees.

The test requires a drawing of a typical tree, so you tell the spectator to draw any tree but a pine tree. To make sure that she draws freely, without fear or inhibition, you also tell her that the experiment isn't about judging her artwork. Beyond that, she's free to draw any way she wants.

Analysis

In the 'Tree Test', the notion of space is different from its meaning in handwriting. In the latter, most signs related to space are evaluated *relative to the writing* itself. In the Tree Test, however, these signs are evaluated *relative to the sheet of paper*, not the drawing. This affects the meaning and interpretation of the signs.

The **size** of the tree indicates **presence**. If the tree seems too big for the page or seems to overflow, the person *stands out*. If it's small and seems dwarfed by the page, the person is *reserved*. Anything in between these extremes indicates *normal* presence.

The **horizontal** position of the trunk on the page indicates **sociability**. If the trunk is closer to the right, the person is very *sociable*, drawn to others. Toward the left, the person prefers *solitude*. Centred, the person's sociability is *average*.

The **vertical** position of the drawing on the page represents the person's **motivation**. If the tree is nearer the top of the page, the upper zone

A little extra...

dominates and the person is driven by the *mind*, ideals. Centred, the middle zone dominates and the person is driven by practical considerations and *emotions*. Low, the lower zone dominates and the person is driven by *instincts* and the *physical world*.

The **slant** of the tree indicates the person's attitude toward the **past and future**. A right slant means that the person is looking forward to the *future*, whereas a left slant indicates that the person is *cautious*, more comfortable with the known, the past. A vertical tree with no slant indicates a *balanced* attitude toward the old and the new.

The **ground line**—the line that represents the earth, even if it's not drawn—is equivalent to the baseline, and indicates the person's **mood**. Rising, the person feels *optimistic*; falling, the person feels *pessimistic*, and horizontal, the person's mood is *even*.

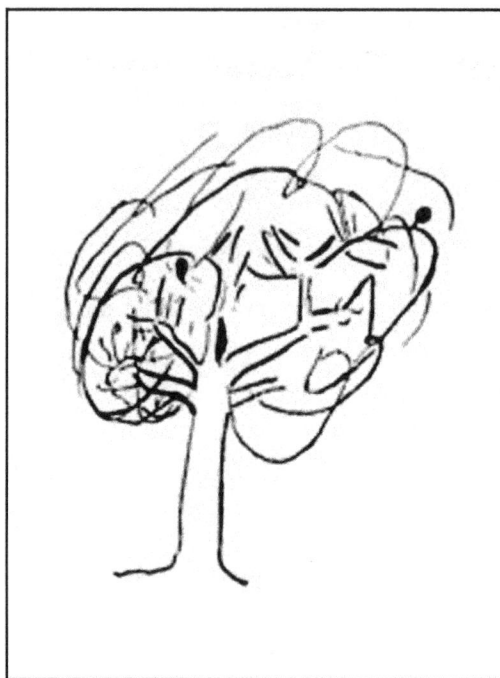

The tree above shows average presence, a preference for solitude, the middle zone dominates, slight enthusiasm for the future, and a somewhat pessimistic mood.

Applications

The 'Tree Test' is ideally suited to readings. For short or strolling readings, the information above is sufficient. For full-length readings, Rudy Hunter's *Draw me a tree* DVD describes a complete system for reading tree drawings as well as signatures.

In a mentalism act, the 'Tree Test' can be presented as yet another version of 'Pseudo Psychometry'. Spectators draw a tree on coded index cards, you interpret the drawings and hand them back to their owners.

The cards can be coded in any of the methods previously described, but here's one that's particularly well suited to this experiment[31]. Get index cards that are lined on one side only and take them to an art supply store, where you buy a blue pencil that matches the colour of the blue lines. Prepare the cards by thickening the very beginning of the line, at the left edge, ever so slightly. You can thicken the first five lines, or you can thicken five lines at even intervals from the first line to the last. In the first case, you count the lines to find the coded value; in the second, you find the value by its relative position. Use the method that's easiest for you. The spectators draw on the blank side; when you hold up a card to show it, you can see the marking clearly.

For a magic performance, here's a trick by our own rising star, Jeff Hinchliffe, who graciously gave me permission to describe it. In Jeff's original version, both the spectator and the performer draw a picture and sign the back of their cards; at the end, the signatures transpose. The version below has been modified to use a single card in order to better fit the story.

PRICELESS ARTWORK

You will need a packet of about twenty or thirty cards that are blank on both sides, a small silk foulard, and one or several permanent markers of different colours, fine- or medium-tipped. To prepare, draw a paw print on the top card, which you then turn over. Place the packet in your left pocket, the prepared card away from your body, together with the foulard. Place the markers in your right pocket or case.

---

31 Devised by Sid Lorraine, described in Bascom Jones' *Magick*.

"*A mystery from the world of art. We'll need a famous artist—that's you... some blank canvases... and a few brushes.*" Pick a spectator near you, but to the side. Bring out the cards; fan them to show that they're blank, being careful not to expose the paw print on the bottom card, then close the fan, flip the packet over and fan again to show the other side. Place the packet on the table, followed by the markers.

"*We need a painting of a tree—it can be any tree you like, except a pine tree. And since you're a famous artist, your artwork will be considered a masterpiece, no matter what, so feel free to draw as you see fit.*" Place the squared packet in front of the spectator, short edge toward her, and if you like, hold the packet in place at the corners farthest from her, ostensibly to help prevent it from shifting while she draws.

"*Let's see what kind of artist you are... I see that you prefer solitude, so you're a famous reclusive artist!*" Pick up the packet and hold it in dealing grip. Look at the drawing and describe a single trait, in the context of an artist.

"*You can actually tell a lot about a person from a drawing of a tree. Psychologists call it the 'Tree Test' and use it to determine a person's character. See, the tree toward the left tells me that you prefer solitude. But your tree is quite large, which means that you like to be in the spotlight too, so you're a famous reclusive artist who enjoys being admired.*" Explain and point out the sign, then do a reading on a second one. Pause for a beat to let the reading sink in.

Lean back and bring the hand holding the packet toward you, to signify that the reading is over. Address the spectator: "*Now let's get back to our mystery from the world of art. We'll need a title for your painting. What would you like to call it?*" Help the spectator, if necessary, to find a name that's a bit longer than simply 'Tree'. Depending on the drawing, the use of colour, and your own preferences, you can suggest, for example: 'Study in Red', 'Weeping Willow', 'Tree in Winter', 'Feeling Blue', or even 'Tree on a Card' or 'Green Tree is Good For You'. While you're discussing this with the spectator, prepare for a double turnover, if you need a get-ready.

Once the spectator has decided on a name, address her: *"Please write that on the back, and your name below"*, and do the double turnover casually, while talking. Place the packet on the table in front of her, this time with a long side nearest her, and hold the packet as before, if you did so earlier.

When she's finished writing, take the packet back, blow on the writing, tilt the packet so the audience can see the face of the card and rub your fingers briskly back and forth across it, ostensibly to check that the ink is dry, but actually to show the audience, subliminally, that the writing doesn't come off.

Address the audience. *"Now the story can begin. One morning in 1892, the chief of the Paris police got a message from The Fox, the notorious art thief, stating that he was going to retire after one last heist. He was going to steal the new painting the next day at noon during its inauguration at the Louvre. The chief of police smiled to himself; finally, he was going to catch the rascal!"* As soon as you start talking, casually do a double turnover and place the top card in the middle of the table, with the tree right-side up from the audience's point of view.

"At the Louvre, the day of the inauguration, the painting was covered with a cloth under the watchful eyes of the chief of police. It was guarded by his best men. Security was tight; The Fox didn't stand a chance." While talking, put the packet in your pocket and bring out the foulard. Open it and spread it on top of the card, then have several spectators hold it in place with their fingertips around the edges.

"Precisely at noon, as the painting was about to be unveiled, a loud 'clang!' came from the kitchen. All heads turned to see what was going on. Quick to react, the chief of police turned to the curator and shouted: 'Unveil it now!' To his great surprise, the painting was exactly where it should be, in full view." Matching the actions to the story, pick up the markers, hold your hand high above the table and to the side, and drop the markers to make the sound. Then, with your other hand, pinch the foulard in the middle, have the spectators move their hands away from it and whisk it away. Drop the foulard on the table to the side.

Lean back. "*The story of the painting ends here. The curator was happy: he had his painting. In fact, it's still hanging in the Louvre today. The mayor and the Paris art world were happy: The Fox was never heard from again. Only the chief of police was unhappy: he was convinced that something had happened that day, but he could never prove it, and eventually gave up.*" Pause for a full beat.

"*Very few people know that he was right to be suspicious. Instead of simply stealing the painting, which would've made the theft obvious, The Fox replaced it with a forgery.*" Pause briefly, then nod toward the card and add: "*See for yourself.*" If necessary, direct a spectator to turn the card over.

Pause until the reaction dies down, then add the tag line: "*You can keep the forgery. The original is in my safe at home... with the rest of my great-great-grandfather's collection.*" Smile enigmatically as you deliver the last part, then segue into your next trick.